D1053341

FEMALE SEXUALITY
AND THE
OEDIPUS COMPLEX

Female Sexuality
and the
Oedipus Complex

HUMBERTO NAGERA, M. D.

Professor of Psychiatry and Chief of the Youth Service
University of Michigan
Training Analyst, The Michigan Psychoanalytic Institute

JASON ARONSON ● New York

ISBN: 0-87668-206-9

Library of Congress Catalog Number: 75-5709

CONTENTS

Classical Psychoanalysis and Its Applications:

A Series of Books
Edited by Robert Langs, M.D.

Female Sexuality and the Oedipus Complex

By *Humberto Nagera, M.D.*

Dr. Nagera brings to clinical psychoanalysis a rich background in both child and adult psychiatric and psychoanalytic work. This is an outgrowth of several years of training in Havana, Cuba; a long stay in London, England, where he held a variety of teaching and research positions at the Hampstead Child Therapy Clinic, and the London Institute of Psychoanalysis; and his current positions in Ann Arbor, Michigan, where he is a training analyst for the Michigan Psychoanalytic Institute and professor of psychiatry at the University of Michigan. Based on this unusual clinical and research heritage and on his own unique capacities as an observer, integrator, and theoretician, he has previously published a series of papers and books on a wide variety of topics. His major papers have been on childhood development, fantasy and ego formation, infancy and adolescence; while his books touch on such diverse topics as developmental psychoanalytic psychology; the basic psychoanalytic concepts of libido theory, dream theory, instinct theory, and conflict and anxiety; and the life of Vincent Van Gogh. His work has provided rich areas of insight for students of human behavior of the most divergent orientations.

His present careful and searching study of the Oedipus Complex and sexuality in the young girl evidences his brilliant researches into important areas of childhood development. It is filled with important implications for the understanding of childhood and adult psychopathology, and the therapeutic strategies and techniques needed to help patients to resolve such pathology. Nagera's work is a vivid illustration of the broad usefulness of clinical psychoanalytic observations and their carefully reasoned implications regarding both normal and pathological development. It is welcomed into this series as an important clinical and theoretical contribution from a highly productive psychoanalyst.

ROBERT J. LANGS, M.D.

FOREWORD

Dr. H. Nagera's book is a welcome reminder of the profitable years spent by him in and for the Hampstead Child-Therapy Clinic. As expressed by him in his own introductory chapter, it was especially his work with the Clinic's Diagnostic Profile and his Chairmanship of the organization's Clinical Concept Group which roused his interest in the limitations which still place the analyst's knowledge of female development far behind that gained of their male peers.

In his approach to the problems of female sexuality, Dr. Nagera is, thus, in a far more favorable position than many analytic authors who have tackled this difficult subject before him. While those who are only analysts of adults have to be content with reconstructing the childhood events which are responsible for the deviations from normality in later life, Nagera, in his additional capacities as child analyst and diagnostician of children, is privileged to see the developmental processes themselves in action. To assess their beneficial or adverse effect for adult sexual behavior, he has at his disposal not only the analyst's familiar notions of fixation and regression, but also the concept of progressive forward moves on prescribed developmental lines.

From firsthand experience and child-analytical cases, Nagera constructs four of such lines for drive development itself and demonstrates the possibility to examine each of them separately as to its intactness or disturbance: change of object, of erotogenic zone, of sexual and of active-passive position. But, possibly more important and also more revolutionary than this, he proceeds to discuss the intimate interaction of these with three other influences which simultaneously shape the individual's sex life: the innate variations in the strength of the different component instincts; the rate of progress on the line of ego development; and the environmental circumstances and experiences which either favor or interfere with orderly developmental progress. With such a multitude of forces at work, he does not find it surprising that the deviations from a normal outcome are as numerous and as complex as they prove to be.

He reverts repeatedly to one particular factor in female sexual development to which he attributes outstanding significance, namely, the absence of a leading erotogenic zone during the little girl's positive oedipus complex. Even after all the other agents in the situation are disentangled from each other, he confesses himself still faced with the question how an organ appropriate for the discharge of masculine-active excitation can be adapted to the same function regarding passive-feminine strivings. He thus sees and describes the girl's sexual life until and beyond puberty as one deprived of an executive organ, a void which needs to be filled on the psychological side by means of mechanisms and processes such as identification, desexualization, sublimation, etc.

While being guided through these developmental vicissitudes, readers can have every confidence in an author who acknowledges the presence of obscurities where our present state of knowledge renders them inevitable and who refuses to simplify matters which are, by nature, complex.

ANNA FREUD

London, 1974

PREFACE

Systematic use of the Diagnostic Profile for both adults and children at the Hampstead Clinic forced my attention to some of the obscurities and difficulties involved in assessing the section of the Profile dealing with drive development, more especially as it concerns the oedipal development of the girl. This development will not only shape much of her character structure and personality in general but will largely determine the nature of her sexual adaptation in adult life and her attitude to men and motherhood. This monograph has developed out of my investigations. Furthermore, it re-examines and brings up to date some aspects of our theoretical framework in the light of the clinical observations that we have accumulated through the years and of recent advances in several fields of science.

The research for this monograph was financed by the National Institute of Mental Health, Washington, grant MH-05683, and was part of the research program of the Clinical Concept Research group at the Hampstead Clinic, a research group of which I was chairman.

I am indebted to all staff members and departments of the Hampstead Clinic for the facilities given for the study of the relevant clinical material and for many of the examples used as clinical illustrations.

HUMBERTO NAGERA, M.D.

FEMALE SEXUALITY
AND THE
OEDIPUS COMPLEX

CHAPTER 1

An Historical Perspective

The development of psychoanalytic ideas about the oedipus complex and female sexuality generally proceeded very gradually. For this reason, terms that were appropriate for the original and more simple formulations became ambiguous, insufficient and at times contradictory when applied to the more complex formulations that arose from further insight and the unravelling of innumerable complications. Unfortunately, when a student or more casual reader selects specific papers from a particular phase in a long line of historical development, he may not be aware that the same terms were being used with connotations entirely different from those of later or earlier papers. Nevertheless, no conceptual difficulties need arise if the student approaches this subject historically, following the development of the concepts gradually over the years. When the historical line is taken, it is usually clear in Freud and others what developments—changes, amplifications, reformulations and the like—have taken place, even though the terminology remains the same.

As the complexity of female sexual development and the female oedipus complex became better understood Freud himself became dissatisfied with the inappropriateness of the existing terminology. Mack Brunswick, who had been collaborating with Freud in the study of these problems, describes his views (1940, p. 235) :

> I should like to offer a suggestion made by Freud in our early discussion of these problems. The terms "active" and "passive" oedipus complex are more comprehensive and ac-

1

curate in their application to both sexes than the usual positive and negative oedipus complex. According to this new terminology, the preoedipal sexuality of the girl becomes her active oedipus complex with the mother as its object. Her passive oedipus complex has the father as its object. For the boy, the active oedipus complex denotes what we ordinarily call the positive oedipus complex with the mother as the object. His passive oedipus complex which we ordinarily term the negative oedipus complex has as its object the father, and is a neurotic phenomenon when occurring to any marked extent (1).

To my mind, even this terminology with its obvious advantages cannot sufficiently characterize the various possible oedipal constellations (see Chapter 2). In any case, the increasing complexity of the subject and the fact that different authors use these terms with more than one meaning, at times even in the same paper, make it necessary to look at the problems involved to attempt a clearer classification and set of definitions.*

Female Sexual Development: Freud's Early Views

Freud had established the existence of the oedipus complex by the summer of 1897), as we can see from his correspondence with Fliess (Freud, 1897).

He described it for the first time in his published papers in the *Interpretation of Dreams* (1900), though he did not use the term "oedipus complex" as such in his published writings until 1910 (Freud, 1910).

From 1897 to 1919 Freud assumed, and so did every other analyst, that the sexual development of boys and girls leading to the oedipal complex was almost identical, the only difference being that the boy took the mother as his positive object while the girl took the father. It was only in 1919 in "A Child Is Being

---

1. For this purpose I have consulted the chapters on "The Oedipus Complex: Definition and History of the Term;" "The Oedipus Complex of the Boy:" The Oedipus Complex of the Girl," in H. Nagera (ed.), *Basic Psychoanalytic Concepts on the Libido Theory*, Vol. 2 in The Hampstead Psychoanalytic Library. New York: Basic Books (1970).

Beaten" that Freud first referred to the significant differences existing in the sexual development of boys and girls. These differences were spelled out slowly and gradually in his later work as his awareness of them increased and as the contributions of other analysts, most especially Abraham (1920), Lampl de Groot (1927) and Helene Deutsch (1925), clarified the situation and influenced his own views and formulations. One important repercussion of early theory was that, despite the later recognition of the "negative" or "inverted" complex, which in the development of the girl precedes the move towards the father, Freud and others continued for some time to use the term "pre-oedipal," reserving "oedipal" for the succeeding attachment to the father. Freud corrected this situation in *On Female Sexuality* (1931, p. 225), but some ambiguity still remained. He said:

> Since this phase allows room for all the fixations and repressions from which we trace the origin of the neuroses, it would seem as though we must retract the universality of the thesis that the Oedipus complex is the nucleus of the neurosis. But if anyone feels reluctant about making this correction, there is no need for him to do so. On the one hand, we can extend the content of the Oedipus complex to include all the child's relations to both parents; or, on the other, we can take due account of our new findings by saying that the female only reaches the normal positive Oedipus situation after she has surmounted a period before it that is governed by the negative complex.

In "From the History of An Infantile Neurosis" (1918 [1914]) Freud does refer to the oedipus complex of the patient as an inverted one and in the *Introductory Lectures* (1916-17) he refers to its possible "variations or its possible reversal," but the general impression one gathers is that these were considered as possible alternatives, and not obligatory concomitants. In fact, up to the publication of *The Ego and the Id* (1923a) it was mostly the "positive" aspects of the oedipus complex that were predominant. In that work, however, Freud makes clear "that the *simple Oedipus complex* [my italics] is by no means its commonest form, but rather represents a simplification of schematization. . . . Closer study usually discloses the *more complete Oedipus complex* [my italics] which is twofold, *positive and negative* [my italics] and is due to the bisexuality originally present in children (2).

Up to this point the terms utilized remained satisfactory and clearly defined the phenomena described. The *simple oedipus complex* referred to what he describes now as the *positive* aspects (in boys and girls) of the *more complete oedipus complex* that included both *positive and negative* aspects.

The "Negative" Complex

The terms only became confused, contradictory and insufficient at the point when further insight led other analysts and Freud to postulate that the girl's oedipal development proceeded in two stages, and that another stage, at which the oedipal object of the girl was not the father but the mother, must be interpolated before she reached what was considered up to that point her oedipal complex (including both *positive* and *negative aspects*). This important contribution was made in 1927 by Lampl de Groot. Four years later Freud (1931, p. 226), following Lampl de Groot, stated that

> the female only reaches the normal positive oedipus situation after she has surmounted a period before it that is governed by the negative complex. And indeed during that phase a little girl's father is not much else for her than a troublesome rival, though her hostility to him never reaches the pitch which is characteristic of boys.

---

2. That Freud took so long to establish explicitly in his written work the link between bisexuality and the oedipus complex with its tremendous repercussions is in itself surprising, if we consider that as early as August, 1899, he wrote to Fliess: "Bisexuality! I am accustoming myself to regarding every sexual act as an event between four individuals" (Freud, 1899). Though Freud and Fliess parted company soon afterwards and the letters remained unpublished until 1950, it could not be argued that Freud buried this insight, suggested by Fliess, with the end of his relationship to him. In the *Three Essays* (1905) he wrote: ". . . without taking bisexuality into account, I think it would scarcely be possible to arrive at an understanding of the sexual manifestations that are actually to be observed in men and women."

It was at this point that the same term, "negative complex," started to be used indiscriminately to describe two very different stages in the development of the female oedipus complex, that is, both the phase of attachment to the mother and the negative aspects of the oedipus complex proper (attachment to father).

At the same time that Freud described the role that bisexuality plays in the oedipus complex he pointed out (1923a) that it was "this complicating element introduced by bisexuality that makes it so difficult to obtain a clear view of the facts in connection with the earliest object-choices and identifications and still more difficult to describe them intelligibly." He advised analysts to assume always the existence of a factor which he was calling at this point the "complete oedipus complex," but which did not as yet include the girl's phallic-oedipal attachment to the mother as the preliminary stage of the oedipal attachment to the father. He added:

> Analytic experience then shows that in a number of cases one or the other constituent disappears, except for barely distinguishable traces; so that the result is a series with the normal positive oedipus complex at one end and the inverted negative one at the other, while its intermediate members exhibit the complete form with one or the other of its two components preponderating. At the dissolution of the oedipus complex the *four trends* [my italics] of which it consists will group themselves in such a way as to produce a father identification and a mother identification.

Naturally, with the later discovery by Lampl de Groot of the new stage (the negative or inverted complex) in the oedipal development of the girl the difficulties of assessment and description increased further. Nevertheless, I believe that an examination of the different lines of development involved in the establishment of the oedipus complex can be very helpful, as I shall show in a later chapter.

With the discovery of the "pre-oedipal" changes in the girl Freud and others, including Lampl de Groot (1947) and Van Der Leeuw (1958), were led to wonder about the possibility of a similar stage in the development of the boy, which, as Freud pointed out, was more or less unknown (1925). Most, however, came to the conclusion that such a phase was specific to the development of the girl. In 1931 Freud stated: "Thus in female development there is a process of transition from the one phase to the other [negative complex to positive complex], to which there is nothing analogous in the male" (1931, p. 228).

The Term "Pre-Oedipal"

A further source of possible misunderstandings arises from the different uses of the terms "pre-oedipus" or "pre-oedipal." Originally this was meant to cover the oral and anal phases of drive development in children. When Lampl de Groot discovered the new phase of the negative or inverted complex, characteristic only of female sexual development, she also described this as "pre-oedipal." Though this usage was incongruous in metapsychological terms, she justified it on the basis that the girl's final oedipal position should normally be a positive attachment to the father, while the phase we are describing preceded it. Freud himself, though only for a short time, as we saw earlier, included this stage as part of the pre-oedipal phase. Thus "pre-oedipal" included in the case of the girl the oral and anal phases as well as the negative or inverted complex. In the case of the boy it included the oral and anal phases and a hypothetical phase that was for some time assumed to exist in the boy as an equivalent of the girl's newly discovered pre-oedipal phase. When it was finally realized that no such phase existed, "pre-oedipal" was once again reduced to cover the oral and anal phases. In short, when this point was reached "pre-oedipal" for the girl included three stages —oral, anal and negative complex—while in the boy only two stages—oral and anal. One can in this instance very clearly see the advantages of approaching the study of this subject historically as the only way to avoid misunderstanding and confusions.

To complicate matters further, this same "pre-oedipal" stage in the girl is simultaneously referred to as the "negative oedipus complex" or "inverted complex." This is unfortunate, because there are two possible negative oedipal constellations in the girl that have in common only the object chosen (the mother); all other significant factors involved are different, as we shall see, since they correspond to two different levels of development. This lack of discrimination in terminology obscures the metapsychological differences between constellations and results, in practical terms, in bypassing or at least misunderstanding substantial aspects of the development of the girl, of her unconscious fantasy life and the psychopathology associated with it.

To my mind, Freud's final decision to describe the negative or inverted complex of the girl as an integral part of the oedipus complex, not as a pre-oedipal phenomenon, is the more profitable approach. It is general metapsychological considerations and not just the object chosen, that ought to decide if the negative or inverted complex of the girl should be termed pre-oedipal, or oedipal. To include this complex within the pre-oedipal stage, as is sometimes done, obscures its more essential characteristics, that is, its phallic-oedipal nature and the fact that for the first time in the girl's development a truly triangular relationship has been reached.

Metapsychologically speaking, there are no essential differences between the so-called "positive oedipus complex" of the boy and the "negative complex" of the girl. In both cases the phallus (in the girl its equivalent) has acquired phase dominance, the sexual position is a masculine-active one, the object chosen is the mother, the degree of ego development and accompanying fantasies are similar, and the level of object relationships and behavioral manifestations generally are more or less identical.

Lampl de Groot (1927) stated this quite clearly.

> She [the little girl], too, takes as her first love-object the mother who feeds and tends her. She too, retains the same object as she passes through the pregenital phases of libidinal evolution. She too, enters the phallic stage of libido development. Moreover, the little girl has a bodily organ analogous to the little boy's penis. . . . Physically she behaves exactly like the little boy. We may suppose that in the psychic realm also children of either sex develop up to this point in an entirely similar manner; that is to say, that girls as well as boys, when they reach the phallic stage enter into

the oedipus situation, i.e., that which for the girl is negative. She wants to conquer the mother for herself and get rid of the father.

Freud fully agreed with this formulation in "On Female Sexuality" (1931, p. 241), stating that in Lampl de Groot's paper

the complete identity of the pre-oedipal phase in the boy and the girl is recognized, the sexual (phallic) activity in the little girl's attitude towards the mother is stated and proven by observation. The whole development is epitomized in the formula that the little girl has to pass through a phase of the "negative" oedipus complex before arriving at the positive one.

Mack Brunswick (1940, p. 251) also comments: "We have seen how closely the little girl in her active pre-oedipal attachment to the mother resembles the little boy in his active oedipus complex."

In Chapter 2 we propose a conceptual approach to these problems that should avoid the confusing situation described above.

CHAPTER 2

The Ideal Normal Development

The generally accepted pattern of normal female development after the anal stage can be represented in diagrammatic form (see Figs. 1 and 2).

First Stage PHALLIC-OEDIPAL	Second Stage OEDIPAL
Positive ↑ MOTHER +++ ♂ FATHER − − − (a)	*Positive* + FATHER +++ ♂ MOTHER − − − (b)
Negative + mother − ♂ father + (c)	*Negative* ↑ mother + ♂ father − (d)

FIGURE 1
For an explanation of the symbols and typography, see page 10.

Figure 1 and Figure 2 (p. 11), which includes a representation of the "inverted complex," are constructed on the same model. At a glance the different positions (normal or abnormal) corresponding to the different developmental stages of the oedipus complex can be characterized in their essential features and components, not only on the basis of the object chosen—a characterization that frequently proves misleading. Thus diagnosis is facilitated, as illustrated below.

9

Both the first and second stages show the two most essential oedipal constellations: the normal position with its positive and negative aspects and, in the case of Fig. 2, the abnormal outcome of the inverted complex as well.

The first stage has been called "phallic-oedipal" because during this stage clitoridal activity is phase dominant, as contrasted with the second stage named "oedipal," when clitoridal activity tends to be suppressed more or less successfully. Though the vagina does not necessarily play any significant role in the second stage, psychologically speaking many passive-feminine identifications with the mother have started to acquire relevance.

In Figures 1 and 2 the squares representing either the positive, negative, or inverted complex at each stage show the object that receives the positive cathexis and its rival, which receives the negative cathexis. Capital letters and three + and — signs represent those objects that receive the greatest cathexis, while those that receive the less significant cathexis are representd by small type and only one + and — sign. The former objects normally receive the cathexis from those elements of the bisexual complex that have the upper hand at a particular point in development; the latter receive the cathexis corresponding to the less important bisexual counterpart. Since it is possible to divert the cathexis (feminine or masculine) to the wrong object, the symbols ♂ or♀ in the squares characterize further the aspects of the bisexual conflict from which the complex arises, and the length of the line indicates which aspect of bisexuality has the upper hand in each one of the constellations illustrated. The ego attitudes, beliefs and fantasies cannot be represented in the diagram but those that correspond to any of the constellations during the first stage (phallic-oedipal) are very similar, at least in a few fundamental essentials. The variations that have been observed are frequently determined by the direction of the cathexis to one or another object and the experiences, environmental situations, etc., that influenced it. The same applies to those corresponding to the second stage, including the positive, negative and inverted complexes. Naturally, second-stage ego attitudes are fundamentally different from those of the first stage. Their characteristics are described in Chapter 10.

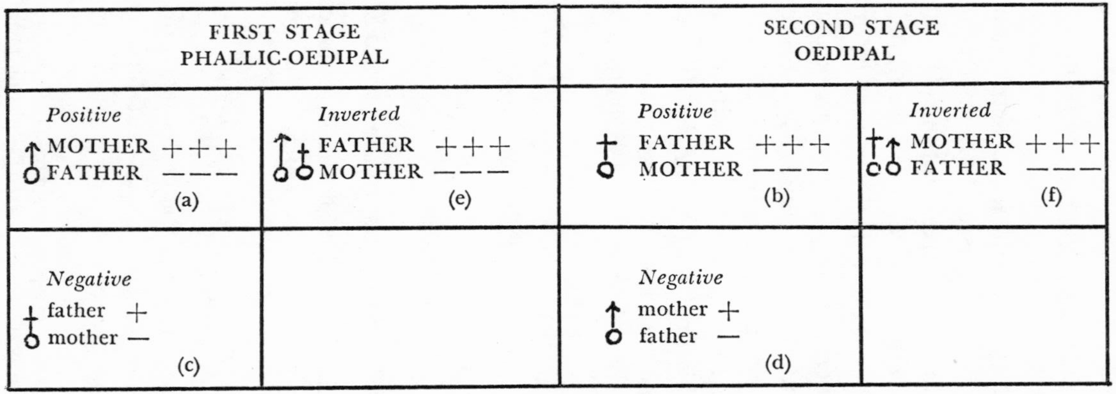

FIGURE 2

For an explanation of the symbols and typography, see page 10.

The First Stage (Phallic-Oedipal)

After the anal phase of development the girl moves into the "first stage" of the oedipus complex, a position that is characterized by the intense cathexis of the clitoris (phallus), which brings about the phase dominance of this specific erotogenic zone. At this point the girl's sexuality is essentially masculine and she is naturally in a masculine and active position (1). She consequently takes the mother as the object of her masculine, active phallic strivings (see Figure 1, square [a]), where the intensity of the rivalry with the father is shown as proportional to the positive attachment to the mother. But though the overall balance at this stage is clearly on the masculine side, the little girl is bisexual, and we have to consider the vicissitudes in the feminine components of her bisexual nature. In the diagram they can be seen cathecting the father as the positive object while the mother is seen as the rival, but they are of relatively lesser importance (square [c]).

From the ego point of view we have to take into account that this phallic-oedipal stage is usually accompanied by the belief that all human beings possess a phallus, including, of course, the mother.

The Move from the First to the Second Stage

The move from the first stage of the oedipus complex of the girl to the second stage involves significant changes in a number of areas. They are:

1. Change of object (mother to father)
2. Temporal suppression or abandonment of the clitoris as the essential erotogenic zone, with later addition of the vagina

---

1. Some analysts took some exception to Freud's formulation of the phallic phase in girls. Thus Jones (1927) stated: "Freud's 'phallic phase' in girls is probably a secondary defensive construction rather than a true developmental stage." Eight years later (1935) he accepted it was something primary with some skepticism. He insisted that the phase was, in addition, a reaction to the girl's dread of femininity, concluding that there is more femininity in the young girl than analysts generally admit. Rado (1931, pp. 460-461), Fenichel (1932) and Horney (1924) also questioned in different forms and degrees the existence of this phase.

3. Change from a masculine position to a feminine one, partly determined by innate factors, partly by certain ego developments
4. Change from activity to passivity (closely related to 3)
5. On the ego side the change requires the abandonment of belief in the universal existence of the penis, the acceptance of its absence in women, including herself, and of substitutes for it (babies), the concomitant reduction of penis envy, the achievement of suitable feminine identifications and concomitant changes in the conception of intercourse and of the fundamental fantasies about it.

The Second Stage (Oedipal)

If all proceeds ideally in these four or five lines (we will discuss later not only normal variations of this but the possible psychopathological vicissitudes that affect the different lines) we arrive at the situation represented as oedipal in Figure 2. There the bisexual balance has changed and the girl largely abandons her previous masculine position for a more passive-feminine one. The object mother is exchanged for the object father, who becomes the recipient of a strong positive cathexis coming now from the passive-feminine aspects of the girl's bisexual constitution. Insofar as there is this strong positive cathexis of the father the mother, who is an interference with it and with the associated fantasies, receives a negative cathexis and becomes the hated and dreaded rival (square [b]). The now less important masculine components of her bisexual nature cathect the mother and the father is the rival for the affection of the mother (square [d]).

CHAPTER 3

An Abnormal Variation

In all descriptions of the different oedipal constellations a number of general assumptions are made automatically. For example, it is assumed that the masculine components of bisexuality have a general tendency to cathect the object of the opposite sex and similarly that the feminine elements tend to cathect the masculine object. Generally speaking this is correct. Yet in the face of certain interferences with development deriving from conflicts or environmental circumstances, these general tendencies are no longer operative and the cathexis can be diverted to objects of the same sex. It is this possibility that explains the existence of the "inverted" complex.

Figure 2 adds to Figure 1 a frequently observed and important abnormal variation in the normal oedipal constellations. Notice that there are two inverted complexes, one in each stage. Since they are completely different in nature it is essential that when we refer to either we specify the stage.

The Inverted Complex—First Stage

The inverted complex, first stage, is characterized by a strong positive cathexis of the father (1) with the mother as a rival, from an essentially masculine position. The ego fantasies and attitudes are those that will be described later as typical for the first stage. (See Chapter 10.)

---

1. Or, of course, the displaced equivalents of mother and father.

14

Second Stage

The inverted complex, second stage, is in contradistinction characterized by a strong positive cathexis of the mother with the father as the rival, from the essentially feminine position. The ego fantasies and attitudes are those that will be described later as typical for the second stage. (See Chapter 10.) The first and second stages are in fact complete opposites in terms of the objects, the sexual position and the ego attitudes and fantasies.

The Negative and the Inverted Complex, First Stage

The Negative Complex

The negative complex, first stage, does not represent anything more than the counterpart of the positive complex, first stage. Its existence is due to the bisexual nature of the girl: the feminine elements of her bisexual constitution cathect the father positively. These feminine elements are, quantitatively speaking, much less important during the first stage than the masculine ones, since the girl is in an essentially masculine position and has taken the mother as the object of her positive masculine cathexis. Thus the negative complex, first stage, is characterized in terms of its objects by a small positive cathexis of the father and a small negative cathexis of the mother. The sexual position is in general the one typical for the first stage—an active-masculine position— but the cathexis that the father receives corresponds to the "minority" feminine elements in the girl's personality. These elements may be identifiable when we observe, even as early as this, isolated examples of rudimentary passive-feminine behavior toward him; these are in fact the precursors of the positive oedipal attachment to the father from a passive-feminine position, which is typical of the second stage. These passive-feminine flashes toward the father are observable amidst the predominant active-masculine attitudes of the girl. They are somewhat obscured for the observer (and for the child) by the confusion introduced by her ego attitudes and fantasies, which are largely of a masculine character.

The Inverted Complex

The inverted complex, first stage, shares the object choice with the negative complex, first stage. In both cases the cathexis is directed toward the father, but in the inverted complex it is not only the minority feminine elements that cathect the father but the quantitatively more important masculine elements as well. Since it is masculine sexuality that is predominant, the girl is in an active-masculine position, and the ego attitudes and fantasies are in correspondence with such a position.

Schematically the similarities and differences between the inverted and negative complexes, during the first stage are as follows:

NEGATIVE COMPLEX		INVERTED COMPLEX	
Object:	father +	*Object*:	FATHER + + +
Rival:	mother —	*Rival*:	MOTHER — — —
Sexual		*Sexual*	
Position:	Generally masculine but the cathexis of the father is essentially on the basis of the *feminine* elements of her bisexual personality	*Position*:	Generally masculine, the cathexis of the father is essentially on the basis of the *masculine elements* of her bisexual personality + sometimes the feminine ones
Ego		*Ego*	
attitude:	Typical of first stage	*attitude*:	Typical of first stage

The Negative and the Inverted Complex, Second Stage

The similarities and differences are as follows:

NEGATIVE COMPLEX		INVERTED COMPLEX	
Object:	mother +	*Object*:	MOTHER + + +
Rival:	father —	*Rival*:	FATHER — — —
Sexual		*Sexual*	
Position:	Generally feminine but the cathexis of the mother is essentially on the basis of the *masculine elements* of the girl's bisexual personality	*Position*:	Generally feminine, the cathexis of the mother is essentially on the basis of the *feminine elements* of her bisexual personality plus sometimes the masculine ones
Ego		*Ego*	
attitude:	Those typical of second stage	*attitude*:	Those typical of second stage

As Anna Freud (1965) has pointed out, in the individual child "one or another oedipal constellation may be emphasized and those quantitative differences can be taken as prognostic indicators for the future. They reveal important preferences for either one or the other sex which are rooted in preoedipal experiences."

CHAPTER 4

Sources of Conflicts and Interference with the Normal Oedipal Development

The normal development of the oedipus complex, especially in girls, is dependent on the harmonious interaction of a multiplicity of factors, which are themselves open to influences of a very diverse nature. It is, therefore, no surprise that the girl's sexual development is of far greater complexity than that of the boy and highly susceptible to interferences and deviations. During the phallic-oedipal and oedipal stages the many developmental stresses intrinsic in the processes characteristic for these phases determine a number of conflicts usually translated into typical and well-known symptoms and behavioral manifestations. When they remain within limits we are in the presence of the normally expected infantile neurosis, itself nothing more than the typical developmental disturbance characteristic of this period of life. Not infrequently the manifestations of the infantile neurosis are beyond the normal limits, an indication that special difficulties are being confronted. The outcome of these may well be to lay down the basis of future psychopathology, owing either to the intensity of the conflicts and/or the influence of unfavorable environmental circumstances, or to the existence of even earlier difficulties, fixations, etc., from the oral and anal phases that will influence negatively the struggles and stresses of the oedipal phase and its resolution. I have described this in detail elsewhere (Nagera, 1966).

A fixation of the first stage of the girl's oedipal development may be determined by any number of factors, acting in isolation or in interaction. They include specific environmental experiences leading to excessive gratification or frustration during this phase, the intensity of the ambivalence toward the mother in the previous anal phase, the strength of the masculine components of bisexuality, the father's attitude to the initial feminine overtures of the little girl, etc.

In other cases where the fixation to the *first stage* (in terms both of the object and the sexual position) is not so marked, the step toward the second stage of the oedipus complex will be taken by all the drive elements that have remained free. Clinically, this results in a mixed picture. It combines in different proportions elements of the first and second stage—the objects cathected (father and mother or their substitutes) by the masculine and feminine components of the bisexual strivings of the girl—as well as other characteristics introduced into the oedipal constellation by the vicissitudes of the five different lines of development. As we know, a normal outcome is dependent on the harmonious unfolding of these lines of development, and naturally the final clinical picture will be partly dependent on the rate of progress that has been possible along them. It is similarly evident that, since development in one or more of the lines can be interfered with at one or more points, there can be any number of variations in the final outcome and clinical manifestations. The significance of the latter must consequently be assessed individually. Generalizations, for example, that a patient has a positive oedipus complex implying a strong positive attachment to the father, are useful as rough guidelines; they establish the type of object choice but do not necessarily convey information about any of the other lines.

A further consequence of the fixation at the first stage is that, in direct proportion to its importance, the child will find it more difficult to reach the second stage and to establish itself safely there. There will be a lesser capacity to tolerate the stresses and anxieties inherent in the higher developmental position; this, combined with the regressive pull determined by the fixation, may lead to a regression to the first stage. A more specific and detailed discussion of the above and other aspects will be undertaken in Chapter 6.

CHAPTER 5

Some Important Variations

There are a number of other possible variations during the first and second stages that deserve consideration.

Move from the Positive to the Inverted
Position, Second Stage

During the second stage, for example, it is possible to observe a defensive move from position (b) to position (f) in Figure 2; that is, from the strong cathexis of the object father with the mother as the rival to the strong cathexis of the mother with the father as the rival. This is frequently referred to in the literature as a defensive or regressive move from the positive oedipus to the negative or inverted complex. It is not always realized that this description is not only insufficient but misleading, since it refers to the vicissitudes of the oedipus complex in terms of the object only, ignoring the other essential characteristics.

Since the *positive* oedipal relationship, second stage, to the father can be highly conflictive, regressive moves from that position are frequent. Most unfortunately, not always in such cases is the attempt made to distinguish between the defensive reinforcement of the negative oedipal constellation, second stage (Figure 2, square [d]) and the inverted oedipal constellation, second stage (Figure 2, square [f]) nor between either of these two positions and a true regression from the second stage to the first stage, that is, to an earlier developmental phase with all its consequences in terms of drive and ego organization, level of object

20

relationships and the type and nature of the corresponding reactivated fantasies, the different intensity of the cathexis, etc. This confusion is facilitated by the fact that in phenomenological terms, in all these cases, there is a positive cathexis of the mother with the father as a rival, as can be seen in Fig. 2 (a), (d), (f). This lack of discrimination must have serious repercussions for treatment: the true nature of the unconscious mental contents and fantasies will escape the therapist, and the wording of interpretations must of necessity be inappropriate. It seems to me very feasible that failures of analytic therapy in some cases of female sexual disturbances such as homosexuality, frigidity, etc., can be accounted for in this way.

The situation is further complicated by the fact that the terminology that is generally used to refer to the different phallic-oedipal or oedipal constellations is ambiguous and imprecise, even at times contradictory. Take, for example, the positive attachment to the mother during the first stage (phallic-oedipal) represented in the figures by square (a). It is variously described as the "inverted complex," the "negative complex," the "active complex," the "phase of pre-oedipal attachment to the mother," etc. All of these terms but the last are indiscriminately applied also to the "negative complex," second stage, square (d). Yet there are fundamental differences between these three positions.

Though I agree that behavioral expressions of the object relationships of the three positions are in many ways similar, it is usually possible, clinically speaking, to make a differential diagnosis among them and to establish the correct oedipal constellation and position of the patient. Such a differential diagnosis will take into account, first, that the overall position of the girl during the *first stage* is masculine, while during the *second stage* it is essentially feminine. In both cases the positive strivings toward the mother and the rivalry with the father are based on the masculine aspects of the girl's bisexuality. Yet in the first case the general background is the masculine-clitoridal position, in the second the general background is completely different, since the girl that has reached the normal second stage has largely abandoned the masculine position and is now in an essentially feminine one. This shows clearly in the small girl's attitudes to objects, games, fantasies and in her behavior generally. It should be noted that a regression to the object mother of the first stage (with the attendant modifications in all the lines) or a move toward the mother of the inverted complex, second stage, may determine, in extreme cases, a homosexual outcome and a homosexual object choice in the adult, either in reality (leading to overt homosexuality) or only in fantasy, crippling the sexual life of the patient. In either case the homosexual position adopted will be in the case of regression to the first stage, an active-masculine one, in the case of the defensive move toward the inverted complex, second stage, a passive-feminine one with special characteristics.

Other clarifying elements include the fact that the manifestations of the positive attachment to the mother during the second stage (Figure 2, square [d]) are of relatively minor importance, when compared with the manifestations of the positive attachment to the father (Figure 2, square [b]), which clearly dominate the picture. During the first stage the situation is the reverse, with the manifestations of the positive attachment to the mother clearly predominant.

The defensive move, (b) to (f), implies that the girl has again made the mother the essential object of her positive cathexis. It does not imply that her feminine position has been abandoned for a masculine one. This would have happened only if a regression had taken place to the positive oedipal constellation of the first stage (position [a]).

In fact the defensive move to the inverted complex, second stage (position [f]) is not, properly speaking, a regressive move, not even insofar as the object cathected is concerned. Even less is it so in regard to any of the other developmental achievements characteristic of this stage. The fact that the object cathected is the mother, as in the earlier phase, constitutes only a superficial resemblance with that stage. The mother to whom the girl is now relating, as far as her ego conception of her goes, is not the same mother of the first stage, the phallic-mother. It is a mother "without a penis" to whom the girl now relates from a feminine position, which she has reached with a genuine move into the second stage of her oedipus complex. Similarly the fantasies about the mother, about the possession of a phallus, about sexuality generally have not necessarily regressed to what they were during the first stage of the oedipus complex, but may well have remained at the level that corresponds to the second stage. In fact the only change consists in the fact that an object that ought to have remained of secondary importance has again acquired predominance.

True Regressions from the Second to the First Stage

A *true regression* from the second to the first stage will on superficial examination present a similar picture to those above, since in this case too the object father is given up in favor of the object mother. Nevertheless a closer look shows that associated with the change of object there is a *real regression* to an earlier developmental position, as demonstrated by the simultaneous change from a passive-feminine position to an active-masculine one, or at least a noticeable increase in masculinity, and by a concomitant reinforcement, through that regression, of some of the ego beliefs, sexual theories and fantasies that correspond to the first stage. This regression from the second to the first stage is uually preceded by a reinforcement of the negative complex, second stage (position [d]). It implies an increase in the masculine elements at the expense of the feminine ones, an increase that is only possible through the regressive reinforcement of the phallic-oedipal stage and the corresponding phallic (clitoridal) erotogenic zone.

Move from the Positive to the Inverted
Position, First Stage

Just as we can observe during the second stage a defensive move from the positive to the inverted complex, we can similarly observe during this stage, a move from the positive to the inverted complex of the first stage. The positive complex during the first stage is characterized by the positive cathexis of the mother (father as rival) from the active-masculine position in which the girl finds herself. In ego terms it is characterized by the beliefs, sexual theories and sexual fantasies described in Chapter 10. The dominant erotogenic zone is the clitoris. *The inverted complex of the first stage* is characterized by the strong positive cathexis of the father with the mother as rival, instead of as the main recipient of the cathexis, still from the same masculine position in which the girl finds herself. The dominant erotogenic zone, ego beliefs, fantasies and theories are similar to those of the positive complex, first stage.

Summary

The move from the positive to the inverted complex of the first or second stage only implies a change of the object; the sexual position (masculine or feminine) is retained, and so is the degree of ego development associated with the achievement in the other lines. A forward move from the first to the second stage or a regression from the second to the first stage imply simultaneous changes in the object and in the sexual position (masculine to feminine in the forward movement, feminine to masculine in the case of regression), and important changes in the dominant erotogenic zone, ego beliefs, sexual theories, sexual fantasies and identifications.

The change of position from the positive to the inverted complex *during the first stage* is perhaps not as frequently identified as it ought to be, partly because attention is paid only to the change of object. Many observers jump to the conclusion when this happens that it is a manifestation of the "positive oedipus complex" (to use current terminology) or of the "positive complex, second stage," in my usage. This is obviously an incorrect assessment, since only the object has been changed and not the sexual position, dominant erotogenic zone or the concomitant ego attitudes.

Such a move during the first stage is determined, for example, by extremely rejecting mothers—a situation that forces the girl to redirect her cathexis to a more receptive father—or, as I have observed in a few instances, it can happen in cases where the mother is absent (divorce, abandonment of home, death, etc.), and the father himself has taken over the mothering role (1).

---

1. The same applies in the second stage of the oedipus complex in the case of absence or death of the father, where the mother takes over or is given by the child the fathering role. Some of these children of course invest some other figure from the environment, teachers, friends, uncles, siblings, etc., with the oedipal role of the missing parent, but some measure of the above is to be observed in every case.

It seems to me that the approach I have taken here helps to throw light, in what is otherwise an obscure and confused area of psychopathological phenomena with a multiplicity of clinical variations. It does so by linking it developmentally with the correct oedipal positions, constellations, and oedipal stages while taking into account the levels reached in the different lines of devolopment.

CHAPTER 6

The Change of Object from
Mother to Father

In both girls and boys the mother is the fundamental object during the anal and oral phases of development. The role of the father at this time is a much less significant one. With the move up into the phallic-oedipal phase, that is, the "first stage" of the female oedipus complex, the father attains a new, special significance that is similar for both boys and girls. He now acquires tremendous importance, in psychological terms, as an active rival in the *phallic sense* for the affection, care and attention of the mother. He is the one felt to interfere in what would be otherwise an ideal relationship between the child (boy or girl) and his mother. As such he becomes the object of the child's hostility, a situation particularly conflictive since by now the father has also attracted some of the child's cathexis and positive feelings. In any case, the child wishes him out of the way, and therefore fears the retaliation in kind of his much stronger and more powerful rival. Hence the intense castration anxiety typical of the phase, more particularly so for the boy. All the above is summarized here only to highlight the vital differences in the complexity of the object relations, conflicts, ego concerns, etc., between this stage and the earlier oral and anal ones.

When the girl moves into the "first stage" of her phallic-oedipal conflict she still retains the object of her previous phase, though her relationship to that object has acquired special characteristics that distinguish it sharply from the same relationship during the

26

anal phase. These characteristics are imposed by the move into the foreground of phallic-clitoridal impulses in the drives, by marked advances in ego development, and by the development of an intensely charged triangular pattern of object relationships (child-mother-father). To give but one example of these "special characteristics" take the child's possessive attitude toward the object. The anal-phase child is of course extremely possessive of his mother, but this possessiveness is more primitive in character and contains many sadomasochistic elements and a wish to have the object under control, while at the same time the child is still subject to violent swings of love and hate according to whether he is gratified or disappointed, etc. The possessiveness of the phallic-oedipal child is on a higher level, not so ambivalent; indeed, children behave and feel like little male lovers to the mother, to whom they have become protective, wanting to take the father's place in the relation to her, etc.

I have intently used the expression "male lovers" because the girl reaching the first stage of her oedipus complex has reached a clearly defined active-masculine position as its precondition. The move into the second stage of her oedipal development requires a number of substantial changes in the drive and ego organization (see Chapters 8 and 10)) as well as an exchange of the object, taking the father as a substitute for the mother.

If all goes well in *all lines* the girl reaches the *second stage* of her oedipus complex. In her further development she still has to accomplish a displacement of the cathexis now attached to the father toward a suitable male substitute. Freud (1924d, p. 178f) expressed the opinion that the girl's appropriate resolution of her attachment to the father remained a doubtful achievement, since they lack the strong motivation that the boy has to abandon his cathexis of the mother as an oedipal object—that is, the threat of the narcissistic injury of castration. It is generally assumed that the girl turns to other objects out of disappointment with the father, who does not respond to her physically or provide her with babies (1).

---

1. If there were reliable data on the frequency of incestuous sexual relationships between fathers and daughters as contrasted with mothers and sons (especially in adolescence), we could have a valuable indicator. From isolated observations

Some Frequent Variations in This Line
of Development

These variations from the general developmental norm are described because of their importance and clinical significance as well as to highlight the complexity of the process involved.

Freud (1915) pointed out that the different instinctual impulses must be considered from the point of view of their source, their aim, and their object. The source and the aim are quite fixed and characteristic for any one of them, but the relationship between the instinctual impulse and the object is very loose, and the object of any given instinctual impulse can and is in fact frequently changed according to convenience. Though on the one hand this is very economical, emotionally speaking, on the other it constitutes in some ways a weak spot in the instinctual organization. It is precisely at this point that the impact of a number of significant environmental influences, the usual developmental conflicts, and those of a neurotic character will make themselves more easily felt.

This distinctive, loose relationship between the drives and its objects is responsible in a number of individuals for the final shape of the sexual organization. It determines constellations that at first sight may appear quite contradictory, since they seem to be in sharp contrast with the basic innate femininity or masculinity of any given person. An example occurs when an essentially "feminine" woman adopts as an object another woman (with phallic characteristics or without them), becoming homosexual. To this group belong those female homosexuals whose position in the homosexual relationship is essentially a passive-feminine one. They have moved normally in the line from masculinity to femininity, but the natural tendency of the feminine cathexis toward a male object has been severely interfered with and has been diverted in the direction of a female object (2). Traumatic

---

and hearsay it would appear that incestuous relations between fathers and daughters are a much more common phenomenon, a fact that could partly be explained by lack of appropriate resolution of the girl's oedipal attachment to the father.

2. Similarly an essentially masculine man may take as an object another man as a result of specific conflicts that misdirect his masculine sexual cathexis. In extreme cases such men become overt homosexuals, usually taking, to start with at least, an active position in the homosexual relationship.

experiences with male objects, the father's massive rejection and disapproval of the girl's oedipal strivings toward him, certain types of fixation to the mother especially perhaps at the oral and anal levels, etc., may determine this development.

Nevertheless, I believe that in most of these cases there is not a complete move into overt homosexual practices. Because of the massive interference with the heterosexual strivings, both in reality and fantasy, a homosexual object choice is made in fantasy. Once this has happened actual sexual behavior can be completely inhibited, or these people may have the occasional, usually unsatisfactory relationship, depending on the intensity of the repressions and on the anxiety and conflicts aroused by such adventures. Clinically, the sexual gratification of these patients is based on masturbatory fantasies, where some sort of a sexual relation to an object of the same sex is the essential element. These fantasies can oscillate between a nearly platonic, amorous relationship to the performance of sexual intercourse with the object in certain specific ways. The exclusivity of the relation to a homosexual object, even in fantasy, is not always absolute. There are in fact many cases where mixed fantasies (hetero- and homo-) are observable in various degrees, with the general balance on the side of the homosexual object. Since this description is as applicable to boys as to girls, I shall use as an example a late adolescent boy I treated:

He was seventeen and a half at the beginning of treatment. In his conscious fantasies he was always longing for a suitable homosexual partner, a wish that led him to visit public lavatories and other places in the hope of a pick-up. In real life he always withdrew, on the many occasions when he was approached by another homosexual. In fact, he had never had an overt homosexual relationship and was somehow doubtful that he could do so in spite of his conscious longings. His sexual life was centered on masturbation accompanied by varied fantasies in which he had a relationship to another young boy, ranging from a platonic brotherly relation to seducing the boy for anal intercourse. He was always the active one, giving the passive role to his sexual partner—

a passive role with anybody was completely repugnant to him. Very occasionally the object selected for the fantasy was a young girl, and in such cases he penetrated her anus, avoiding altogether the vagina. Insofar as he was consciously interested in women (only to a small degree) "they had no front," only their backs were of interest to him. This fact, coupled with the disgust he felt for the female genital organs, clearly showed the intensity of his castration anxiety. The whole thing led to a near denial of the existence of an anterior part of the female body.

Generally speaking, this type of case has a better prognosis than other forms of homosexuality or sexual disturbance in men (and women) where, apart from the misdirection of the object cathexis, the basic position retained or adopted (masculine or feminine) is not the appropriate one.

It will be evident by now that the case of an essentially "feminine woman" that takes another woman as her object cannot be explained on the basis of a fixation to the "negative oedipus complex," in reference to the *first stage* or to the negative aspects of the *second stage,* because both of these are masculine positions. A fixation to the *first stage* always implies that the girl's development in the line from masculinity to femininity has been arrested in the masculine position. The negative constellation of the second stage of the oedipus complex is based in the masculine elements of her bisexual nature.

When a female has reached an essentially feminine position in the line from masculinity to femininity and the feminine cathexis are directed to the wrong object, i.e., the mother (as in the case described above), the masculine elements of her bisexual nature may occasionally follow the same direction, cathecting the mother too. This is so especially when the conflicts that determined such misdirection concerned fundamentally the cathexis of the male object *per se.* This can happen, for example, in cases where the father rejects the overtures of the girl, when she fears the hostility she experiences toward the mother when she takes the father as a positive object, etc. Alternatively, if the conflict that misdirects the cathexis is based on the fear aroused by sadomasochistic fantasies of what the male does to the woman (to the passive partner) in intercourse, it is still possible that her masculine cathexis will reach the object father (or any other male), since what is feared is a relationship to males as the passive-feminine partner but not as an active-masculine one.

The Fixations and Their Role in the Outcome

The nature of the earlier oral and anal developmental phases affects, of course, how the first and second stages of the oedipus complex (and the corresponding objects) are reached and maintained. It is essential to take into account whether the fixations that may have occurred as a result of the vicissitudes of any of the earlier phases affect essentially the drive organization, the object relations, or both. I think that clinically there are important differences here. Taking the oral phase as an example, we can see patients where the oral fixation affects more fundamentally the drive organization and where sexual gratification is fully dependent on the stimulation of active participation of the oral erotogenic zone. An extreme example of this can be observed in cases where the practice of fellatio constitutes the main and perhaps the only source of sexual gratification, as in the case of some perverts. What is essential here is the stimulation and gratification of the oral zone, the practice of fellatio *per se*, and not the object. In fact, any object will do for the purpose. Similar but less extreme cases, where the direct sexual aim has been diverted, can be seen in those cases of overeating, the fundamental factor is the food, the excitation of the oral erotogenic zone and the gratification of that excitement through sucking, chewing, eating, etc. In all these types of cases there is a certain detachment and distance from the objects, in striking contrast with other orally fixated patients who have special and inappropriate expectations from objects. They adopt a passive, clinging and demanding attitude as if they were helpless and required protection and care as a small infant and the object's attitude to them than on the activities of the oral erotogenic zones themselves. It would seem implicit that the second type of patient has reached a higher degree of development and integration. He is less self-sufficient and more *object-oriented* than the first type, whose oral manifestations are closer to those observed during the initial phase of autoeroticism (Nagera, 1964a) and to the self-sufficiency of the autoerotic activities and forms of gratification, e.g., adult thumb-sucking. In fellatio, for example, the object is necessary but its presence is incidental to the practice itself and has no real significance.

In short, a fixation to any phase of development may be auto-erotically oriented or object-oriented. Clearly, these are the two somewhat artificial extremes, and the large majority of cases will show different combinations of autoerotically oriented and object-oriented phenomena. In the latter instance, we find cases who demand from the object the direct gratification of the erotogenic zones involved.

The *object-oriented* type of oral fixation will interfere with the normal move of the cathexis to the appropriate objects. At every new stage the object cathexis is directed toward those objects that may satisfy the existing oral dependence. In the case of the little girl it is rather unlikely that such a figure will be the father, a situation that complicates her move into the positive attachment to the father (second stage). When the fixation involves the direct gratification of the oral erotogenic zone it follows that much of the energy that should support the later and more advanced phases of drive development will not be available for the purpose. Conflicts at the higher levels and more especially at the oedipal stage take place, then, against a background of weaker organizations, and, through the pull exercises by the oral fixations, may induce a regressive move. This move cannot fail to have serious consequences for the normal unfolding of development, which becomes impossible, and psychopathological solutions and symptom formation result.

The Role of the Anal Sadistic Fixations
and of Ambivalence

The influence of all these variables in the general sexual development of the girl is well established and requires no further elaboration here. I shall refer only to the special difficulties that confront the little girl when she attempts to substitute the father for the mother as an object during the second stage of her oedipal development if she was during the anal sadistic stage more than usually ambivalent toward her mother.

In normal (and abnormal cases) the usual ambivalent feelings present in the anal phase (especially toward the mother) are partly resolved by the strong positive cathexis directed to her during the "first stage" of the phallic-oedipal phase of the girl. This intense cathexis is perhaps one of the factors behind the process of "fusion" that is observed with the move from the anal-sadistic into the phallic-oedipal phase. This view is supported, on the other hand, by the fact that girls that have shown extremely ambivalent feelings toward the mother during the anal phase find a great measure of relief in this respect at the time they move into the *first stage* of their phallic-oedipal phase. On the other hand, it is these same girls that find it particularly difficult to enter fully into a positive relationship with the father (*second stage* of their oedipal development). Of necessity, this relationship turns the mother again into the hated rival, bringing back in full strength the earlier ambivalent conflicts toward her.

In a number of the cases observed at the Hampstead Clinic the retreat from the positive attachment to the father was due to this problem. Furthermore, we have observed some striking examples where the retreat was quickly triggered by a death in the family. Such an accidental event seemed to bring into the foreground a great deal of the anxiety arising out of the rivalry, hostility and death wishes toward the mother characteristic of this phase (3). The regressive abandonment of the positive attachment to the father (second stage of her oedipal position) avoids the dangers and anxiety provoked by the rivalry with and death wishes against the mother. Furthermore, the regression to the *first stage* of the oedipal constellation further protects the

---

3. In one such girl treated at the Hampstead Clinic by E. Dansky, it was the death of a rabbit belonging to her older sister, to whom she had displaced most of the oedipal rivalry to the mother, that determined the regressive move from the positive oedipal attachment to the father (second stage) to the positive oedipal attachment to the mother (first stage). In the case of this seven-year-old girl the fact that father did not encourage the girl's positive strivings toward him also contributed.

mother by making her again the recipient of a strong positive cathexis. Not infrequently, we have noticed that an inability to separate from the mother ensues at this point.

In our experience, this group of girls is usually quite incapable of completing their oedipal development and consequently their normal development into womanhood without the help of treatment. These cases remain arrested in an infantile position—the first stage of the oedipus complex—not because of an important fixation at that level (the fixation is in fact at the anal-sadistic stage) but because of the intensity of the conflict confronted when the next developmental step is taken. In the move away from that higher stage many of these girls do not regress to the stage where the fixation point lies—the anal stage—as is usually the case, but to an intermediary position, the first stage of the oedipus complex. By so doing the ego avoids the conflicts at higher and lower levels, but only at the expense of an arrest in the development of the personality. In this way the attachment to the object mother perpetuates itself.

CHAPTER 7

The Active-Passive Polarities

I need to clarify my usage of the terms "active" and "passive," "active-masculine" and "passive-feminine," before I can discuss the lines of development from the active-masculine position to the passive-feminine one. I believe that the very loose use of these terms in the literature not only obscures many essential issues, but hinders progress and understanding of the factors involved.

Activity and passivity are nowadays rather loosely equated by many respectively with masculinity and femininity. Reference to an "active" woman frequently implies a phallic, rather masculine woman, to a "passive" man implies strong feminine leanings in his personality. What can be questioned in this usage is not that activity frequently coincides with masculinity or passivity with femininity, but that it does not allow for the fact that "active" and "passive," "activity" and "passivity" have at the same time wider connotations, for example, some of the behavioral manifestations of the aggressive drive, or certain ego styles of coping. It therefore seems essential to me to determine with exactitude if the *sexual position* adopted by children (in infancy), or by an adult, woman or man, during sexual intercourse (or in their fantasy life) is *passive* in the sense of wanting to be penetrated and possessed by the object. In this exclusive sexual context, passivity equal femininity, and equally *active,* implying wanting to penetrate and possess the object, again connotes masculinity.

35

The Active-Feminine Male

We are familiar for example with certain types of male homo-sexuals in whose overt behavior there is nothing that will suggest their basic femininity (or passivity). They not only look and act masculine, but in their respective fields, in industry, politics, business, profession, etc., are formidable opponents, dangerous competitors, giving the strongest impression of "active" people. If in their cases this "activity" were to be equated with masculinity, as is frequently the case, we would be making a serious mistake in our assessment. In their sexual life they may be feminine, the only source of their sexual gratification being through a passive-homosexual role, with the wish to be penetrated, pierced and possessed by their sexual objects. In fact, they can be described as *active-feminine*. "Active" here really connotes the organization and form of expression of their ego's styles and aggressive drives (and not the sexual ones) and *feminine* the adopted, preferred, sexual position.

The Active-Feminine Female

There are many women who in their professional activities or even in their roles as housewives give an impression of "masculinity" because of their "activity"—their efficiency, competitiveness, drive, thrust, etc.—who nevertheless in their sexual life are perfectly capable of adopting a "passive" feminine position. The source of their sexual gratification rests in being penetrated by the penis and possessed by their partners in sexual intercourse. It may be granted that many women showing this degree of competitiveness and "activity" are frequently masculine in their sexual outlook, but this cannot be considered by any means a general rule. Unless we exercise discretion in such superficial assessments we would be driven to conclude that all highly efficient and competitive women are masculine. Clinical observations will sharply contradict such an inference if the position that these women adopt in their sexual life is taken into account. This group of women is best described as *active* and *feminine*.

The Passive-Masculine Male

There are men who will generally be described as "passive," a description that in behavioral terms may well be correct: it is applied to rather shy and withdrawn men who aim low in life, are contented with little and will avoid any competitive situation. In many such cases their passivity is the result of important feminine elements in their personality structure. Yet this cannot be assumed to be so in every case, at least not to such a degree that their basic *sexual position* has been changed from an active-masculine to a passive-feminine one. In a number of such men this "passivity" is due to conflicts essentially centering upon the aggressive drive and to certain ego characteristics and identifications with some aspects of their early objects. Yet in analysis there is no question that many of them have achieved and maintain an essentially masculine position sexually, with no more than the usual normal feminine admixture. They should be more correctly described as *passive* and *masculine*.

The Passive-Masculine and the Passive-Feminine
Sexual Positions

I propose to use the term "active-masculine" instead of "active" when the implication is that the basic sexual position adopted, consciously and/or unconsciously, and the associated sexual fantasies, consist of the wish to penetrate, pierce and possess the object, either by the man (a normal sexual position), or by women (an abnormal sexual position). Similar "passive-feminine" in this context implies the wish to be penetrated, pierced or possessed by the object. This will be the normal position for women, abnormal for men. The terms "active" and "passive" are thus freed from these particular connotations, and can be used for relations that exist between the aggressive drives, different ego styles of coping, and activity and passivity.

Problems of the Active-Passive Polarity

Loewenstein, stimulated by a conversation with Bonaparte about her investigations into the passive phallic phase of little girls, was led to propose on the basis of his own clinical observations a subdivision of the phallic phase for the boy into a passive and an active stage.

The passive stage manifesting itself first and according to my own observations, it actually includes a period of the oedipus complex. Indeed, the sexual aims of the little boy's incestuous wishes are clearly passive, although they may exist side by side with the active aim of penetration which begins to make itself felt at the same period [1934].

Loewenstein puts forward very convincing clinical evidence to support the passive stage—e.g., some forms of disturbances of potency that can be understood as regression to genital behavior the aim of which is passive. He points out that in such cases there is a persistence or increase of passive forms of genital satisfaction. Certain types of male homosexuality may be the result of a fixation at this passive phallic stage, such as those where no anal wishes or gratification play a role but where sexual gratification is on the basis of having the penis touched by the partner's penis. Presumably one could include here as well other types of sexual disturbances where being masturbated is the essential aim. The object in this case may be a woman, as frequently happens with men that are impotent in intercourse, but will respond to masturbatory caresses, or a male, as with some homosexuals whose interest lies in mutual masturbation.

Bonaparte (1953, pp. 42-45) refers also to the exchange with Loewenstein, which confirmed her belief in the existence of a passive phallic stage in the girl, though what she has in mind is essentially different from Loewenstein. She considers that the phallus has a long, passive prehistory comprising the period from the beginning of life to the active oedipus complex. This is the "primary phase" of phallic passivity. The "secondary phase" coincides with the passive oedipus complex (positive attachment to the father). In between these two there is, as if sandwiched, the "active phallic phase," a phase that coincides with the phallic-oedipal attachment to the mother from an active-masculine position. As "proof" of the prehistory of the passive phallus in women she names the predilection of many females for clitoridal caresses.

Mack Brunswick (1940, p. 293) follows Freud (1923b) in considering the three pairs of antithesis—active-passive, phallic-castrated, masculine-feminine—that exist through the entire drive development "mingling, overlapping, and combining, never wholly coinciding, and ultimately replacing one another. Infancy and childhood are characterized by the first two, and adolescence by the third." The first polarity governs the beginning of life when the child is by the very nature of things passive to the active mother. She considers that:

> Normal development demands that activity supervene over passivity whether the passivity remains, is given up, or is converted, we do not know. Clinically it appears to give place to activity. The degree to which this occurs is immensely variable. The process is more vigorous in boys than in girls and the actual quantity of activity is undoubtedly greater. The earlier character of the child depends largely upon the relative proportions of activity and passivity.

She further considers that with the organic awakening of the phallus a period of great sexual activity starts, with passive and active aims present simultaneously. "The libidinal desires towards the mother, both passive and more especially active, become intense. They are accompanied by phallic masturbation with the clitoris as the executive organ of the girl. The boy seems to pass with relative ease out of his predominantly passive, preoedipal attachment to the mother into the characteristically active, normal oedipus complex." She keeps to Freud's suggestion that "active" and "passive" during the pre-oedipal stage are not associated with the sexual distinction (masculine-feminine), inasmuch as the latter does not yet exist.

As we can see, the different authors refer to different aspects or dimensions of the active-passive polarity. I think that four essential aspects of it at least should be distinguished to avoid misunderstanding.

1. The *active-passive* that covers the *activity* of the mother in tending the *passive* child at the earliest stages is an active-passive that belongs more in the realm of general characteristics. As Lampl de Groot says (1952)

Where a feminine surrender is indispensable for a healthy love life, the bringing up of children requires a strong activity, a harmonious blending of active and passive behavior. . . . In regard to her children, who are in need of the actively and passively caring and loving mother, the woman utilizes the attitude resulting from identification with the pre-oedipal mother image.

But since during this time the active-passive polarity does not as yet coincide with the masculine-feminine polarity, I believe that the connection in this case with the sexual drive organization is limited and the phenomenon is fundamentally determined by the immaturity and helplessness of the child at the beginning of life and the role of the mother as the caring agent and is based upon ego attitudes and early identifications.

2. The relation of active-passive with the aggressive drive organization involves quantitative and qualitative aspects as well as certain ego attitudes and identifications.

3. The links between the active-passive polarity and the sexual position (i.e., masculine-feminine) are established at a later stage in development, but never before the phallic phase. They start during that phase and presumably are not fully completed until puberty or thereabouts.

4. Most instinctual impulses have potentially an active and a passive counterpart and aim, a potentiality that becomes an actuality at specific points in development or when in the presence of special circumstances. Obviously one or the other is predominant for any given instinctual impulse, more especially so during specific phases, though its counterpart always exists and in pathological conditions may acquire the upper hand.

Taking into account these considerations, and granting that nobody can escape the significance of Loewenstein's observations, one is forced to wonder if the phenomenon described by him really justifies the formulation of a clearcut passive-phallic stage as a regular phase in the development of the boy that precedes the active-phallic phase. Only more systematic research, including not only reconstructions from adult analysis but direct observations can finally settle this question. Nevertheless, to my mind, at least for the time being, Loewenstein's observations can be sufficiently explained by point 4, above. All that has happened in the cases he describes is that the passive aims have acquired a predominance that in normal conditions they ought not to have by the time the phallic phase is finally reached. Further, it will be important to determine if this predominance is a phenomenon intrinsic to and resulting from the phallic phase itself or has been determined by the reinforcement of pre-oedipal passive trends and the pre-oedipal relationship to the mother, an area upon which Lampl de Groot (1947) and Mack Brunswick (1940) have thrown some light. The passive aims have normally a special importance during the prephallic stage and for as long as phallic dominance is not established. As Mack Brunswick stated, as soon as the phallic stage is reached and phallic dominance established the active aims, in boys and girls, dominate the picture in spite of the persistence of many passive elements that could, of course, become exaggerated.

CHAPTER 8

The Change from the Active-Masculine to the Passive-Feminine Position

These lines of development have to be considered together since there is the closest association between the masculine and feminine positions and the underlying clitoridal and vaginal organization and erotogenic zones. One can generally observe that with the move of the drive organization from the anal erotogenic zone to the phallic zone (clitoridal) and with the concomitant predominance of phallic strivings, a *true masculine* (*active-masculine*) *position* of special significance has been reached. On the basis of the phallic strivings both girls and boys feel the impulsion to penetrate, to intrude, to pierce the object, though the impulse remains vague and undefined, since, on the one hand, the girl's clitoris is not an appropriate object to carry out that impulsion, and, on the other, both boys' and girls' egos have no clearly defined knowledge of the vagina at this point. Furthermore, there is usually for a short time at this stage a universal belief in the existence of the penis in every object. It is this imbalance between the drive development and the ego knowledge (and advances) that explains the type and content of many of the sexual theories of children during this period (see Chapter 10).

Bisexuality and the Phallic-Oedipal Phase, First Stage

It is not always sufficiently understood or emphasized that the move into the phallic-oedipal phase has great influence upon the phenomenon of bisexuality and consequently upon the final establishment of a true masculine position in boys and girls, for the first time in their development. In fact, bisexuality acquires a new significance at this point, becoming fully relevant and operative in the organization of the sexual and fantasy life of the individual. Of course, manifestations of our bisexual nature and tendencies are present from the beginning of life, and can be observed in operation long before the phallic phase. They influence the child's disposition, behavior, likes, dislikes, games, attitudes, etc., to extents that make possible a relative evaluation of bisexuality even at the toddler stage. At that time we can notice that some boys have a more masculine disposition than others; similarly with girls. Furthermore, such innately different dispositions partly determine the special significance of the early environmental events and experiences that a particular child may be subjected to.

Nevertheless, in the earlier phases there was no special discrimination as to the object that was to receive the masculine or feminine cathexis. The personality was not as yet organized in these terms, since, quite apart from the level of drive development, ego development was such that the interaction of the drives and the ego led to a special type of object relationship with one fundamental object, the mother or her substitute. All other objects are usually seen as an interference with this more primitive mother-child relationship if they come in any way between the child and its mother. But whatever the reason for the younger child's conflicts with anything or anybody that interferes with the relationship to the mother, bisexuality seems to play no significant role. The mother seems to receive all or at least most of the cathexis available to the child for some time. With the move into the phallic phase and the concomitant development of the ego, the figure of the father is brought to the foreground, owing to an increasing awareness of his importance and his special relationship to the mother. Thus, there is a redistribution of the child's cathexis—as Anna Freud (1965) states, "In contrast to the preceding stages, the sex of the object becomes of great importance in the phallic phase." This redistribution is now largely determined by the bisexual nature of the child. Normally at this stage the mother receives a masculine cathexis and the father the feminine aspects, giving place to the familiar triangle relationship of the oedipus complex, positive and negative (first stage) .

The Active-Masculine Sexual Position in Boys and Girls

Since, developmentally speaking, the phase reached is essentially a masculine stage with the masculine element clearly predominant, girls and boys both have reached an *active-masculine sexual position*. From this position both take the mother as the essential object. The father becomes the rival in the relationship resulting from this cathexis. Insofar as little boys and girls are bisexual, some feminine elements are present, and these cathect the father as the positive object, with the mother as rival in this relationship.

Naturally any important fixations at the earliest stages of drive development, of object relations, etc., will weaken the phallic oedipal organization that is in the process of being established and handicap the child's ability to cope with the normal developmental conflicts of this phase. If these early conflicts prove too strong or are reinforced by a set of unfavorable external circumstances regression may well be the result, and the basis has been laid for arrests and distortions of the normal developmental processes of the child (see Lampl de Groot [1952], Gittelson [1952], Deutsch [1952], and Nagera [1966a, b]) .

It is possible at this point that if the mother is not available or is an unsuitable object the masculine cathexis of the girl may be misdirected to the father who takes the mother's place. In this case we are in the presence of the inverted complex, first stage.

Some Possible Sources of Interference

The move from the active-masculine position to the feminine one can be interfered with if a fixation takes place to this first stage of the girl's phallic-oedipal development, and the girl remains fixed in a masculine-clitoridal-active sexual position. This fixation does not of necessity imply that simultaneous fixation to the object mother (that is, to the *normal* object during the first stage) has to take place, though this is very frequently the case. In a number of cases, and in spite of the fixation in a masculine position, the father is cathected. The fact that the father (or males generally) are taken as objects can mislead the observer into assuming that the girl has reached the second stage of her oedipus complex or has moved away from the active-masculine position. The second stage implies, as we have seen, not only a change of the object mother for the object father but a simultaneous abandonment of the masculine-clitoridal-active position, with the establishment of at least a psychological feminine identification.

Women with partial frigidity (vaginal anesthesia but not clitoridal) may suffer from this fixation. As Bonaparte (1958, p. 3) says "they are not only the most obdurate to treatment, but also the most frequent."

What I have in mind here is not the old and to my mind obsolete argument of vaginal vs. clitoridal orgasm, but rather a basic psychological attitude where the vagina is a welcoming receptacle (or not) for the penis during sexual intercourse, with all the positive (or negative) psychological implications associated to this, as well as its influence in somatic responses.

The vagina, though a poorly innervated organ, is an integral part of a complex anotomo-physiological sexual mechanism during intercourse, that leads to an orgastic discharge, which is in itself neither vaginal nor clitoridal but due to massive reflex vasoconstriction.

Clearly, in many women this mechanism is interfered with by the wrong kind of psychological attitudes or conflicts about sexual intercourse or sexuality generally, so that no orgastic discharge takes place through the agency of the penis in the vagina during sexual intercourse. Yet, these same women are frequently capable of an orgastic response by means of clitoridal manipulation.

Clinically, we are well aware of all this. An extreme example of this can be observed in some cases of vaginismus. In many more cases the psychological interference simply blocks the possibility of an orgastic discharge through sexual intercourse (the so-called vaginal orgasm).

These facts make it clear that the girl has not reached the second stage, properly speaking, but is in an intermediary and deviationary position more akin to the first stage than to the second.

The Homosexual Outcome as a Form of Interference

Other cases fixated in the masculine-clitoridal-active sexual position are simultaneously fixated to the object mother and consequently retain her (or other women who, in later life, take her place in the sexual interest of the patient) as the object of their sexual strivings. The larger the amount of the drives that remain fixated at this point, the clearer, in clinical, behavioral and phenomenological terms, are the extreme masculine position and the intense hostility, envy, rejection and disgust for men, in sexual terms, of this group of women. The best example is given by those female homosexuals for whom sexual gratification comes almost exclusively from the performance of the active-masculine role in the homosexual relationship. Although they are representative of an extreme group they are by no means rare, though frequently the *polymorphous perverse* facade of the sexual relationships between female homosexuals may hide their existence. This type of homosexual patient may, for example, play what looks like a passive-feminine role in her sexual relations to gratify the needs of the homosexual partner when this is required of her. But this position is not at all a source of sexual excitement, gratification, and discharge for her. Gratification and discharge are completely dependent on her being allowed to play the active-masculine role (1).

---

1. Many factors peculiar to the conditions under which most sexual relationships between homosexuals take place tend to obscure, for the casual observer, the real nature of their sexual organization in general and in terms of their oedipus complex, and of their sexual requirements. Nevertheless, it is only through an appropriate assessment of all this that we can determine the true nature of their fixations and conflicts.

Many homosexual relations are in the category of the so-called "one-night stand." A male homosexual patient described this situation very vividly. When he felt the urge for sex and picked up a partner, his sexual excitement and gratification was dependent on his partner's allowing him to caress his body all over, sucking the partner's penis, and finally anal intercourse. Though an active role

The Modification of the Active-Masculine
Clitoridal Strivings

To complete the move into the passive-feminine position a wave of repression must usually dispose of or at least suspend the masculine-clitoridal strivings.

Experience shows that in the vast majority of cases the addition to the clitoris of the vagina as an essential erotogenic zone does not take place immediately after the rejection of the masculine-clitoridal sexual strivings. In fact, there may be a situation of suspension, before the vagina takes its role as an essential erotogenic zone, until the pubertal period. In other cases this change does not occur until some experience of sexual intercourse has been acquired and in still others until after the birth of the first child. Yet in spite of this, the girl has adopted a feminine position *in the psychological sphere,* with healthy feminine identifications, as some of the clinical examples will demonstrate. These identifications are for the time being purely *psychological,* and the erotogenic zone of the vagina is not, as yet, making a significant contribution; *in this position a large proportion of women remain fixated.*

---

in anal intercourse was his main source of sexual gratification, he himself was disgusted by the idea of being penetrated by anybody, as indeed were many of his occasional pick-ups. Nevertheless, he allowed penetration, and other practices essentially uninteresting or even repulsive to him, if he thought that only in this way could he get from the partner what he desired most, that is, to penetrate him and ejaculate in his rectum. This tendency to compromise seems a general attitude in one-night stands among experienced homosexuals. In the case of my patient and of many other homosexuals this type of relationships is regarded as highly unsatisfactory, and is searched for only occasionally when the internal pressure to have sex becomes so great that they will make a temporary compromise to obtain relief. The situation is different in the case of lasting "homosexual marriages" where a basic condition seems to be that needs are to a great extent complementary and the partners are satisfied with their respective sexual roles.

Clearly, it is not sufficient to assess the true sexual position and oedipal constellations of homosexuals on the basis of the manifest homosexual behavior. It is essential to determine as well the nature of their fantasies, fixations and the type of practice from which they derive their real sexual satisfaction. Furthermore, in a large number of cases there is, simultaneously with these fixations (themselves of varying degrees), a move forward of larger or lesser amounts of the drive organization that accounts for the multiplicity of clinical variations.

The best example of this type of fixation is the large number of married women whose enjoyment of their sexual life is rather limited (at least by the traditional standards), with a consistent absence of orgastic experiences. Yet these women's describe their sexual life rather positively, since they highly value being desired and possessed by their husbands, as well as the pleasure that they provide him. Their gratification is essentially of a psychological nature. They clearly feel they are fulfilling their roles as a female and wife and have an intense degree of psychological satisfaction, with no complaints about the fact that their own sexual pleasure is in many cases close to negligible.

With the move into the second stage, the girl changes from the previous active-masculine sexual position to the passive-feminine one she ought to reach, once she is well established in the second stage of her oedipus complex. Naturally this does not happen suddenly, but slowly and gradually. During this time the girl is not well established in any of the two sexual positions, and oscillates between them. Such oscillations find appropriate expression clinically and behaviorally, a fact that complicates the assessment of the little girl's oedipal position during this particular period. With this change into a passive-feminine position a number of similarly significant changes take place simultaneously in the ego (see Chapter 10) and in the line of object relations (see Chapter 6), where normally the father substitutes for the mother as the positive object. In my view, even more important than this change of object is the simultaneous change of the sexual position from the predominantly active-masculine one of the first stage to the predominantly passive-feminine of the second stage. This means that the bisexual development is unfolding satisfactorily and that neither innate factors nor environmental circumstances have determined important arrests, fixations or deviations in this area.

All going well, the girl reaches the *positive constellation* of the second stage of her oedipus complex with the father as the object of the positive cathexis, cathexis that come from the now predominant passive-feminine components of her bisexual nature. There are of course minute manifestations of the negative constellation, itself the expression of the active-masculine side of the girl's bisexual nature. What must be insisted upon is the nature of this passive-feminine position. It implies, to start with, suppression or an important diminution of the active-masculine strivings, in the psychological sense, plus a number of passive-feminine attitudes and identifications, mostly in the psychological realm, without as yet a very active participation of the vagina. This comes later and only gradually through a number of complicated physical-maturational advances to be described later. The final, fully developed passive-feminine position is still years away. It is of interest to note in this context that the importance of the role given by Deutsch (1925, p. 166) to the penis in the awakening of the vagina finds confirmation in the work of Masters and Johnson (see Appendix).

In the move from the first to the second stage the girl may change her sexual position from the active-masculine to the passive-feminine without the normally concomitant change of object. In this case the girl moves to the *inverted constellation,* not the positive, in the second stage of her oedipus complex.

The addition of the vagina as an erotogenic zone to complement the clitoris, on which the change from the masculine to the feminine position and normal sexual development are so dependent, especially in psychological terms, remains an obscure step and poses a multitude of problems, complicated by our lack of understanding, until recent work by Masters and Johnson of clitoridal function (cf. Freud, 1931, p. 228). Some of them deserve examination at this point.

We do not know of any anatomical or physiological changes that could help to explain the suppression of clitoridal sexuality, as is sometimes implied. The clitoris suffers no anatomical involution and in neurophysiological terms it remains a richly innervated erotogenic zone. It seems to follow then that the suppression of clitoridal sexuality of the earlier active-masculine type is based upon pure psychological factors and conflicts. Prominent among them is the envy, not only of the size of the man's phallus, but because the clitoris, though as highly excitable an organ as the phallus and subjected to the same impulsions to penetrate the object, is incapable of fulfilling such aim.

Though clinical observations tend to confirm the general tendency toward the suppression of this type of clitoridal sexuality at this point in development, it is nevertheless true that in many cases, perhaps in the majority, this is only partially achieved.

In the cases where this repression is too successful, sensuous pleasurable feelings are no longer translated into an excitation of the erotogenic zone. The sensuous feelings nevertheless may still find expression in the psychological realm and can be observed in situations where, for instance, the girl takes a feminine role toward the object, looks after him, admires him, etc. As mentioned earlier, a number of women who enjoy their roles as housewife and mother, but who get little or no pleasure from the sexual aspects of their marriage, belong in this group. To them sexual intercourse is performed as another of their multiple duties and for the benefit of the husband.

What seems to me to be closer to the truth, and frequently overlooked, is that in a large number of girls, what is suppressed is *the active and direct pursuit of clitoridal excitation* through direct stimulation, manually or otherwise (open masturbation, rubbing against objects, pressing the thighs hard together, etc.). Nevertheless, in most cases the clitoris remains an active erotogenic zone that becomes sensuous and excited when the little girl is aroused sexually by fantasies, exciting games, physical contact, etc. Thus the sensuous excitement is *passively experienced* to different degrees in this erotogenic zone; all that has been given up is the *active, direct stimulation of the zone.* It should be noted too that such changes involved a move from autoerotic self-sufficiency to a dependence on the object (a fantasy object or real object) for sexual gratification.

Though there is some discussion as to how early in the life of girls the vagina becomes an erotogenic zone, it seems to me very unlikely that it does so before puberty, or at least to any important degree (2). The vagina and other accessory organs do go

---

2. There has been much argument through the years about the role played by the vagina in all these processes early on in the life of the girl. Freud, Deutsch (1925) and others seem inclined to believe that the role played by it at the early stage is negligible with perhaps occasional exceptions. Brierley (1932) has pointed out the frequency of vaginal contractions during the suckling period. Many other analysts such as Horney (1933), Müller (1932), Klein (1932), Greenacre (1950) and Kestenberg (1956a, b) believe in the existence of early vaginal activity. Kurt Eissler (1939) in an interesting paper surveyed the literature for reports of cases

through a process of anatomical and physiological development that culminates at puberty. The cells of the mucous membrane and glands acquire the adult characteristics during adolescence, as do the Bartholin glands whose secretions occur in response to sexual excitement through fantasies or actual erotic play.

The importance of physical maturation is usually somewhat neglected in psychoanalysis. I believe that maturational changes play an important role in the psychological organization of the sexual life of women. For example, through the maturation and functional readiness of the Bartholin glands the girl experiences a new and concrete physical sensation in her genital organs as a response to sexual excitation. She feels "wet." It is of interest that some women, especially those who are unable to reach an orgasm, not infrequently equate their suddenly "becoming wet" with the male ejaculation and orgasm. A few of the cases I have observed referred to it as having "ejaculated" and assumed that this was their orgasm, showing the identification of their sexuality with masculine sexuality. These women were not completely frigid, they were able to derive a certain amount of sexual pleasure in their contact with men generally and during sexual intercourse, but this pleasure never built itself up into a normal orgastic experience. In fact, their sexual excitement remained at the sensuous level usually associated with the forepleasure activities in sexually normal women—a degree of excitation that is sufficient to bring about the lubrication of the vagina as a preparation for intercourse proper, leading finally to an orgasm. They thought of themselves as normal in their sexual capacities, having concluded that what they experienced was all there was to be experienced in their sexual relations. This was possible because some of these patients had not only completely repressed their wish to masturbate, but all memories of any earlier orgastic experiences accompanying it as well.

---

where objects have been introduced in the vagina of little girls by themselves or others. His findings in this respect are of great interest. He stated: "The cases discussed here perhaps allow one to conclude that discovery of the vagina is possible before puberty or sexual intercourse, even without seduction or anomalous constitution. I can, however, by no means agree with all arguments of those authors who attribute to the vagina an important role in infantile sexual development."

Observation of the conditions of adult female sexuality forces one to conclude that in all normal cases and in the large majority of not so normal cases the clitoris has a substantial erotogenic role. Strictly speaking, among the women who claim orgasm during sexual intercourse only a small number does so through a "vaginal orgasm" (3). Many seem to require the stimulation of the clitoris as a precondition of the final orgastic experience— orgasm is reached only on those occasions where such a stimulation has taken place. I do not mean only manual stimulation or practices, though in many occasions this may be the required precondition. I refer too to the preferences for certain specific positions during intercourse where, quite apart from the excitement aroused by the associated fantasies, there exists the further possibility of a greater stimulation of the clitoris and neighboring areas either directly, or indirectly, through the preputial-glandar mechanism.

It is well established that the location (higher or lower) of the female genital organs in the perineal regions differs among different races: even women within the same race vary, basically owing to the different types of pelvis possible. It seems that the amount of physical stimulation of the female genital by the penis during intercourse will be partly dependent on such normal variations, as well as upon differences in the location of the penis, size, type and angle of the erection, etc.

It is to be regretted that on the whole we are still quite in the dark as to the possible role, psychological as well as anatomical and physiological, of these variations. Systematic research into all these possible normal variations and their role in sexual adaptation is to my mind a matter of highest priority. In the last few years some remarkable research in this area has been undertaken by Masters and Johnson (1966). Sherfey (1966, p. 51) comments: "It is predicted that all future developments in the psychoanalytic

---

3. A consideration of the problems involved in frigidity is outside the scope of this monograph. For a good review of the subject the reader may consult Moore (1964). See also Bonaparte (1953, p. 3), and Sherfey (1966, p. 78), who, on the basis of recent biological evidence concludes that "it is a physical impossibility to separate the clitoral from the vaginal orgasm as demanded by psychoanalytic theory."

theory of female psychosexuality will be biologically grounded in the inductor theory of primary sexual differentiation and in the observations of Masters and Johnson on the sexual cycle in women" (4).

One has to agree with Sherfey's statement, especially if one takes into account:

1. The role the clitoris still plays in most cases in adult female sexual life
2. The lack of significant anatomical or physiological changes brought about by development that could justify a diminution of its importance in later female sexual life
3. The fact that suppression of clitoridal sexuality is a psychological achievement, an ego achievement

It seems that qualified acceptance of the role of this erotogenic zone in normal female sexuality is necessary. The development of normal female sexuality depends not on the exclusion of the sensuous feelings of this erotogenic zone *per se,* but on the suppression, or at least the neutralization, of its masculine character and the masculine-active sexual fantasies associated with it. It is this latter aspect of clitoridal activities that constitutes an obstacle to normal feminine development. If we accept this view, the "vaginal orgasm" can be understood as one of many possible variations of normal sexual adaptation in women. In achieving this neutralization (or even feminization) the ego plays an essential role (1) through the repression of the active masculine fantasies and strivings; (2) through its final acceptance of the lack of the penis and the "inferiority" of the clitoris; (3) through the establishment of suitable feminine identifications and the giving up of penis envy, etc.

It is this step in the development of the girl that I consider particularly dangerous. With the attempt at neutralization or sup-

---

4. Sherfey's paper contains a summary of many aspects of Masters and Johnson's work that are relevant to the psychoanalyst, especially the nature of the orgasm in women and the sexual cycle that leads to the orgastic experience. She brings up to date relevant embryological advances and examines bisexuality in the light of the modern inductor theory of sexual differentiation. Though one may not always agree with her inferences, her paper is an outstanding piece of scholarly work (see also Appendix).

pression of the active-masculine fantasies that accompany the phase of phallic (clitoridal) dominance, it easily happens that the erotogenic zone itself is barred by the ego. When this takes place it deprives the female genital organization of an erotic area that still has an important contribution to make to female orgastic capacity even after the accompanying masculine ego fantasies have been abandoned.

Thus there is a natural link between the psychoanalytic theories presented here and recent anatomical and physiological findings.

These facts, as understood at present, suggest not that the vagina takes the place of the clitoris, but that it comes to integrate itself in well-defined ways with it.

With physical maturity the vagina and more especially the lower third of it comes to form a part of a complex anatomic structure integrated by the vagina (lower third), the labium minor and the clitoris including the clitoral glans, hood and shaft. During intercourse the thrusting movements of the penis provoke mechanical pressures that are transmitted to the clitoris, resulting in friction in the hood, glans and shaft (the labial-preputial-glandar mechanism) that is the main source of erotic sensations leading in time to the orgasmic experience. The actual contribution of the vagina in terms of sensations is minimal. Its contribution in psychological terms is a different matter and requires further explanation if an answer is to be found to some remaining puzzles, such as the preference generally expressed by women for "vaginal orgasms."

CHAPTER 9
Bisexuality

We have been used to consider men and women as opposite poles, in terms of sexuality. From certain angles this is correct but the bisexual nature of human beings makes some reservations necessary. Few people will argue with the concept of "psychological bisexuality," which finds support in well-known and well-established anatomical, physiological and endocrinological facts, but the psychological significance of the differences among men and women remains obscure and unexplored.

From the embryological, anatomical and physiological point of view these differences are very marked. Embryologically, the fetus, whatever its original condition, has a potential capacity to develop either set of organs, masculine or feminine. After the first few weeks development, determined by the genetic code, proceeds ostensibly toward femininity or masculinity. This process shows notable differences in men and women. What is destined to be the clitoris in the case of feminine development evolves to become the penis in the male. The clitoris is a well-developed anatomical entity, richly innervated and highly sensitive, not an atrophic residue. The other elements of what would have constituted the masculine sexual apparatus do not develop or develop into specific structures of the female genitalia. In men, in sharp contradistinction with females, what were destined to be feminine organs develop into specific masculine structures or *become completely atrophic,* leaving minute "scar" tissue by the prostata with no innervation and consequently without feeling or sensation. It

55

seems to me that anatomically and physiologically speaking, the bisexual constitution of women is more of a fact than that of men. This to my mind is in no way contradicted by recent findings leading to the hypothesis that the sexual organs of mammals are, to start with, anatomically and physiologically female structures that can go straight into feminine development or be transformed into male sexual organs by hormonal dictates, as Sherfey (1973) points out. In summary, the primordial embryo is a feminine matrix with the potential to develop into a female or a male. A "male," on the other hand, is the final outcome of this bipotentiality. In itself it lacks, biologically, bipotentiality.

Consider, for example, the relevant anatomical and physiologifactors brought to light by Masters and Johnson's research into the sexual act and the orgastic experience. In anatomo-physiological terms it can be said that the clitoris is permanently contained in its own "vagina." The female orgasm is largely dependent on the mechanical friction between the clitoris' shaft and the glans and the clitoris hood that involves it; this latter, then, performs especially during intercourse, the role in relation to the clitoris that the vagina performs in relation to the penis.

The implications and repercussions of such anatomo-physiological factors in the psychological development of women, and more especially in their sexual development must be tremendous, but are not as yet clearly understood. It seems possible, for example, that the significant differences between boys and girls, in the active-passive balance and in expression of impulses, especially during the phallic phase, may be partly related to this fact. The boy's phallic impulses lead him to search for the "vaginal complement" while the similar impulses of the girl are perhaps partly satisfied by the clitoridal hood.

It is perhaps for these reasons that we observe, quite apart from the general manifestations of bisexuality common to both boy and girl, an active-masculine phase that is specific to the development of the girl and that acquires phase dominance. The boy can, because of his bisexuality and the vicissitudes of his development (interaction of innate factors and environmental circumstances, etc.) *arrive* or *not* at an essentially feminine-passive position. But such an outcome is an abnormal exaggeration of his bisexual nature, itself a deviation from his normal development and not a necessary, regular and normal, phase-dominant stage of it. It thus seems possible that the bisexual nature and the psychological bisexuality of women have special dimensions of their own that contribute to make the sexual development of the female more complex and lead to the high frequency of sexual dysfunctions that we observe.

I am led further to speculate about the nature of the "maternal feelings and the maternal abilities" of women and to wonder if they are not partly based on these differences from men, as well as on cultural attitudes and expectations about the behavior of the sexes. The special dimension of woman's bisexual constitution may well be at the basis of her ability to have the most intimate and, normally, harmonious physical and psychological relationships to her children of both sexes, a natural ability and disposition that no male, not even those described as very maternal, can ever hope to match. Many of the maternal functions and the pleasures derived from them, such as giving the breast to her babies, boys and girls, may be facilitated by these differences. The performance of such functions is completely alien if not repulsive to the conscious mind of the average man.

Finally we should consider that the influence of these anatomical and physiological differences between boys and girls, in terms of bisexuality, is further reinforced by the fact that the mothering functions, naturally, are the responsibility of the female sex (1). For the boy this is a convenient situation, fitting perfectly with the needs of his psychosexual development. For the girl this introduces an added difficulty in her psychosexual development generally and her oedipus development in particular. For her, the cathexis of the feminine mother from an active-masculine position has to be only a transitory stage and not the culmination of her psychosexual development, as is the case with the boy. That the object to which the active-masculine cathexis is directed is a female is clearly advantageous to the boy. Yet it might well reinforce the girl's masculine identification, a position that has to be

---

1. As Lampl de Groot rightly points out (1952, p. 3): "In the life of men a real repetition of the situation of the archaic child-mother entity never takes place, in contradiction to the woman's life, wherein she becomes a mother herself."

abandoned for the sake of normal development. This is so because the unconscious of the mother herself, if of a feminine nature, may encourage the girl's masculinity at this point, quite irrespective of the mother's conscious ego attitude to the masculinity of her daughter. Simultaneous analysis of mothers and their children will throw some light onto these problems, and will highlight as well the role played by the type of oedipal constellations characteristic for any given parent, especially that of the mother and its influences at this stage in the developmental processes of the child.

A Clinical Example

One case treated at the Hampstead Clinic illustrates the mother's reaction to the little girl's overtures to the father. The patient was twelve years of age at the time of her analysis. By that time all the evidence pointed in the direction of an important fixation at the phallic-oedipal position (first stage), to which she had regressed. In so doing she had again taken the mother as the object of her positive, active-masculine strivings. This was best illustrated by her rich fantasy life, especially at bedtime, when she saw herself as a boy having all sorts of masculine adventures. During the period of analysis she was able to recall many memories from the times when she was moving into the oedipus complex (second stage), a position from which she had since regressed. She remembered longing that father would pay more attention to her as well as going to great lengths in order to be noticed by him. She recalled also how excited she used to feel as a small girl when in the company of her father. It was on several such occasions that the mother sent her out of the room to "calm down," because she was jumping up and down, pulling her skirt up, or dancing in front of her father to attract his attention. Presumably, the mother could not tolerate the competition of her daughter. Presumably, too, another factor contributing to the regressive move the patient took was connected with the little attention that the father was able to pay to the seductive overtures of the girl.

CHAPTER 10

Ego Development

The ego of the child has, naturally, an important role to play in the developmental advances that we are describing. The final shape of the oedipal constellation is partly dependent on the level of ego development reached, its general characteristics and on its advances during this period.

The move into the phallic phase widens the level and complexity of object relations and introduces into the ego organization a number of new dimensions. They lead to, even force, great advances in its development and functional capacities.

In the early stages, the events in the life of the child are mostly significant, processed and understood, in the context of a one-to-one relationship, essentially of course the relationship to the mother. From the phallic-oedipal phase onwards, events for the first time have to be elaborated consistently in three-dimensional terms—child, mother and father. Coping with situations in terms of three permanent and simultaneous variables and the multiplicity of possible combinations widens the ego functionally.

With the onset of the phallic-oedipal phase in girls and boys and the concomitant changes in the drive organization, that is, the move of the main body of the cathexis from the anal to the phallic (clitoridal) zone, the ego interests and attention change too and concentrate into the new dominant erotogenic zone for this phase.

Many children have had plenty of opportunity to make observations early in their lives concerning the anatomical differences

59

between the sexes. Yet, in most cases the psychological impact of these observations on children remains limited (except in special circumstances) because the main body of their cathexis, ego attention and interests are concentrated at this time not in the genital area but in the anal erotogenic zone, in the anal processes and the accompanying ego fantasies. Anything outside the interest of the dominant phase is, in relative terms, of secondary importance to the ego of the anal child. Nevertheless, he may well have verbalized observations made during the anal stage by pointing out the presence or absence of the penis in male or female siblings, friends, parents, etc. Occasionally some further curiosity and questioning may accompany these comments and observations. Still, other children take much less notice of all this prior to the phallic phase.

With the developmental move into the phallic phase the situation is completely reversed. Even many of the child's early observations, which at the time seemed to have had little or no effect on him, acquire new meaning and have a powerful psychological impact, in retrospect (1).

With the new cathexis of the phallus (or clitoris) the child's sexual curiosity reaches new heights (2).

The little girl's ego and that of the boy will now and for some time to come carry a great deal of "research" concerning the differences she observes between herself and others. In this way she is led to formulate any number of hypotheses, well known to us in the sexual theories of children, many of which are of necessity faulty. On the one hand, the ego is strongly biased in its researches by the intense wish of the girl to possess a penis.

---

1. The situation created is similar to that of an art lover who, having noticed with mild interest a painting in a market, buys it for a few dollars and hangs it in some obscure corner of a wall at his house. There it remains for years with only the occasional nearly accidental glance. Suddenly one day he discovers the true identity of the neglected painting as a Rembrandt. From that moment his whole cathexis goes to that painting; every detail of it, whatever concerns it, becomes important. From then onward he starts to live in constant concern that it may suffer the slightest damage or that it can be taken away from him.

2. There are cases, of course, where even before the phallic stage the little girl starts to question very intently her previous belief in the similarity of everybody else's body to hers. This is so, for example, when the birth of a male sibling stimulates prematurely (during the second year of life), her penis envy.

On the other it lacks the necessary information and experience to arrive at the right conclusions. Thus, for some time the little girl may cling to the belief that her penis has still to grow further or that it is hidden insde her, etc. But the ego cannot ignore completely, without serious psychopathological consequences, the observations it has made, nor fully accept its own tentative explanations. The seed of doubt is there. It is clearly observable in sets of alternative fantasies where the girl fears that her penis has been taken away or damaged, perhaps as the result of her masturbatory practices.

Usually, the girl's normal and logical belief that all other bodies are anatomically identical with hers is easily shattered by her observations of the male penis. Yet a healthy ego acceptance of the absence of the penis in females is not only a complicated but a slow and gradual achievement. To start with, the observation of the male penis stimulates the girl's penis envy to different degrees, depending on favorable or unfavorable environmental circumstances that interact with factors already present in the child's personality; some of these are innate, others have been acquired through development, and still others are sociocultural in nature. Naturally, the arousal of strong penis envy does not favor the ego acceptance of the absence of the penis, but rather, at least at the beginning, the proliferation of fantasies (leading in some cases to fixations) that will tend to deny it.

Generally speaking, the following sequence holds true, under favorable external and internal conditions: The sight of the male organ causes the girl to develop a number of sexual theories to account for the facts. She concludes frequently, as mentioned earlier, that her penis has to grow (3), that it is hidden inside, etc., while at the same time suspecting that hers has been taken

---

3. One of my adult patients, after observing the father's penis in childhood, developed the fantasy that everybody was born like her, a girl, and that in later life everybody developed a big penis like her daddy. As a little girl, she used to carry with her her own picture and that of her father, telling people, "This is how I am now, but that is how I will be when I grow up."

Rado (1931) has described the organ the girl gives herself in fantasy, when she chooses to ignore the evidence of her senses and imagines that she has a penis, as "the illusory penis." He considers this phenomenon not a simple reaction to penis envy, but a narcissistic reaction formation of the girl's ego.

away, usually by the mother, or that she herself damaged it through masturbation. It is to this latter level of ego fantasies that many women return later on in life during pregnancy when they are suddenly assaulted, at times overwhelmed, by fears that their babies will be born with some abnormality. Obviously some fantasies are overdetermined and commonly reinforced by the existence of significant ambivalent conflicts and conflicts around aggression. Nevertheless, the analysis of these fears and fantasies never fails to discover the important link with the unconscious belief that they have damaged themselves through their masturbatory practices. Just as they had concluded that they damaged themselves, or lost their "penis" through these practices, their babies, as the unconscious substitutes for the penis, are assumed to be damaged too.

These childhood theories imply that for a time, at some stage of her development, the little girl believes herself to be different from everybody else. In other words, everybody else but her possesses a penis, including of course her mother.

Soon afterwards, if factors that could determine a fixation at this level of development and type of ego fantasy are not operative, she will come to terms with the fact that human beings are divided into two groups, those who possess a penis and those who do not. To the second group belong both she and her mother as well as other little girls and women (4).

Through the continuation of her research and her increasing awareness of the role the father plays in giving the mother babies, coupled with her dissatisfaction with her clitoris, and the resentment felt towards the mother who has failed to provide her with

---

4. What is not sufficiently realized sometimes is that side by side with the ego's acceptance of those facts, which it cannot escape, there remains a great deal of uncertainty and puzzlement in the little girl's mind about the reasons for the differences between the sexes. To be told at two or three years of age that "people are born different in this respect" is, of course, useful for the little girl and may contribute to alleviating the guilt accompanying the fantasies of having damaged herself, but it has to be taken on trust. The ego itself is not yet developed to the level where it is capable of a real intellectual understanding of the complexities involved. Because of this and because of the magnitude of the cathexis of the clitoris, of the intensity of the emotions, ego feelings and envy accompanying it, we can see in the same child for some time sets of contradictory theories, some acknowledging the facts, some denying them.

the valuable organ, the girl arrives at the compromise solution described by Freud and others. She exchanges the wish for a penis for the wish for a baby (or babies) that she hopes to get from the father. This solution is greatly facilitated by the simultaneous processes of repression of clitoridal sexuality and of identification with the passive-feminine role of the mother. This, in normal cases, gradually leads to changes in the girl's conception of the relationships between men and women, in the conception of sexual intercourse and in the concomitant fantasies. All this favors a reduction in the girl's penis envy and allows for the displacement of the exhibitionistic tendencies from her phallus (clitoris) to her body and her general appearance, a fact that in ego terms is translated into the acquisition of new ego interests such as looks, clothes, adornments, etc. It is these and similar factors on the ego side, coupled with the further developments of her drive organization, that finally determine her move from the first stage of the phallic-oedipal position to the second stage, taking the father as her object.

Clearly, many of the newly acquired ego interests, attitudes, theories, fantasies, patterns of object relationships, etc., are nothing more than the translation in ego terms, the form of expression at ego levels, of the normal developmental changes that are taking place in her drive organization and in the conflicts around bisexuality. But development is a complex two-way process, and just as internal changes in the drive organization find immediate translation in ego terms, and (through the ego) in the type and nature of object relationships, so changes in the ego itself (through growth, experiencing and learning) and the environmental experiences to which it is subjected can influence drive developments (see also Nagera, 1963, 1966). To give but one example, the identification with a passive-feminine mother that is required if the step from the first into the second stage of the oedipus complex is to be achieved successfully is, of course, an essential aspect of the move from the active-masculine to the passive-feminine position, and influences the change of erotogenic zone. Whatever interferes with this identification, for whatever reasons, will complicate the normal oedipal course. Adequate developments on the ego side will further and partly determine the development of the drives into the appropriate paths.

The significant role played by the ego in these processes constitutes at the same time one of the important weak spots of development. It leaves the ego particularly open to environmental influences and attitudes of the most diverse nature, frequently of a negative character. We have further to take into consideration that the ego's interpretation and response to environmental influences at the phallic oedipal stage are partly determined by innate factors, such as the original bisexual balance and the variations in the strength of the different component instincts, as well as the form in which the personality has been structured during the early pre-oedipal phases (5).

A passive-feminine identification requires, on the one hand, that suitable figures be available at the appropriate time and, on the other, that the life experiences of the girl will not preclude such identification or make the girl feel that it is undesirable or even dangerous. If the mother happens to be not a passive-feminine figure but an active-masculine one, difficulties are bound to arise. Not infrequently too, the girl's passive-feminine strivings are ridiculed and discouraged by her mother. Consciously or unconsciously she resents the oedipal development of a daughter who is then suddenly felt as a threatening and dangerous rival for the affection of the father and other male objects. In these cases the feminine development of the daughter reactivates in the mother her own unresolved oedipal rivalry with her own mother or siblings. Similar feelings on the part of the girl can occur if her early and still tentative passive-feminine identifications and the accompanying overtures to the father are discouraged by him.

Even when the child has a suitable passive-feminine mother to identify with, difficulties may arise if she has been exposed, for example, to traumatic experiences that make her fear womanhood. Early traumatic sexual assaults, brutal treatment of the mother by the father, traumatic observations of primal scenes, pregnancy or childbirth (or even excessive or inappropriate information) may have this effect.

---

5. "Innate" is used here in Martin James' sense (1960) that is, as inborn givens plus early experiences that combine with the inborn factors and modify them.

The vicissitudes of the earlier phases of drive development, when unfavorable, may interfere with the possibility of passive-feminine identifications. For example, important anal-sadistic fixations contaminate the phallic-oedipal stage and force on the child a frightening conception of intercourse that in later life finds expression in fear of relationships with men and more especially in fear of sexual intercourse. Usually two sets of fantasies are observed in such cases, though one type or the other may predominate in any given patient.

One set of fantasies *concerns the pain, or damage that the patient will suffer in the male's hands during sexual intercourse.* An example of this follows:

One of my female adult patients suffering from an inordinate fear of intercourse and pregnancy had one significant unconscious fantasy, the starting point of which could be traced to her early childhood, in her third year of life. The content was as follows: During intercourse the male urinated inside the woman and it was for this reason that a pregnant woman's abdomen grew so big. For years she had felt uncomfortable at the sight of the large abdomen of pregnant women. Unconsciously she was terrified that the abdomen (her own or that of the pregnant women she saw) could burst out if its holding capacity was not sufficient or the male urinated excessively into it. This fantasy, or, more properly speaking, this sexual theory from her childhood remained active and effective in her unconscious till adulthood. The fact that in the meantime she had acquired an exact factual knowledge of sexuality did not in any way alleviate her anxiety, coming as it did from unconscious repressed sources. At the time the fantasy was originated her mother was pregnant (a fact which stimulated her sexual curiosity) and used to play with the patient with ordinary balloons. As she recalled it, the balloons were inflated with air till they exploded with a big bang or were filled with water from a tap until a similar result was achieved.

The immature ego of the child saw in this game a model on the basis of which she tried to understand what actually happens in intercourse, pregnancy with its growing abdomen, and childbirth, especially since she had heard comments about water coming out during the latter.

This example illustrates a piece of sexual research carried out by an infantile ego. Irrational as the results may seem to the adult, if we take into account the ego's immaturity and limited capacity of performance, its insufficient experience and information about the facts involved, the irrationality disappears. In fact, the ego proceeded quite logically in its circumstances. The relative immaturity of the ego when children are faced with this type of developmental conflict is another of the weak spots in the development of the personality.

A further question of interest here is why, of the multiplicity of sexual theories children arrive at, some remain more active and important than others, influencing further development and creating or contributing to the increased intensity of conflicts in later life. In the case just described, the fixation to this specific fantasy was facilitated in part at least by the mother's pregnancy and by the information that her sibling to be was growing up in her abdomen. This stimulated the little girl's jealousy, resentment and hostility against the mother and the new baby. These feelings found an outlet and symbolic representation in the wish that the mother would burst out like the balloon, thus getting rid of the baby as well. I believe that it was the intense guilt associated with this fantasy that contributed to its fixation. In the patient's adulthood it was reactivated when she wanted to get married and to conceive children. Unconsciously she now feared that what she had wished for the mother and unborn child, would happen to her and her baby.

The other possible set of fantasies we were referring to earlier is sadistic in character. In this latter case, *the female patient fears the damage she so wishes to inflict on her sexual partner.* It usually involves damaging or killing him, depossessing him of the penis by biting it off (with the mouth or the vagina), retaining it inside the vagina, cutting it off, etc. Such fantasies may be conscious or unconscious.

According to some of my observations, when the fear of intercourse is conscious and leads to avoidance, it is usually accompanied, at the unconscious level, by strong masochistic or sadistic fantasies and wishes. It is the unconscious wishes that these patients are really terrified of. The conscious fear is only one form of defense against them. In contrast, there are patients with no conscious acknowledged fear of intercourse who nevertheless give the impression of having unconscious frightening fantasies about it. The dread of intercourse in these cases is deeper and based in repressed traumatic events, fantasies or misinformed sexual theories of childhood and not in sadomasochistic elements that have to be defended against by the avoidance of sexual relations.

On the whole it can be said that the right measure of masochism, especially of the type described by Freud (1924) as feminine masochism, favors the ego processes leading in the direction of passive-feminine identifications, while an excessive amount of masochism or its counterpart, sadism, may interfere with such processes (see example, pp. 68-73).

We know from clinical observation that the ego can remain fixated to one or more sets of fantasies of these types. Quite apart from their role in later situations of conflicts, they can lead, according to their type and intensity and especially when in combination with other factors, to abnormal fixations, or developmental deviations in the line from masculinity to femininity, or in the line of object change. In turn this affects the normal oedipal development and in extreme cases determine abnormal oedipal constellations.

Furthermore, the existence of earlier unresolved conflicts and fixations may to different degrees contaminate the phallic-oedipal phase, as we have already explained. It may determine, for example, an anal-sadistic conception of sexual intercourse and thus influence the form of expression of the conflicts at the phallic-oedipal level. The ego is in this way forced to cling to primitive and infantile sexual theories which of necessity interfere with its sexual performance at an adult level. Ego interests and behavior generally will be influenced as well. It is for these reasons that many of the conflicts typical of the phase are expressed not only in phallic-oedipal language but in oral and anal terms, a situation that can further confuse the judgment and assessment of the inexperienced observer (Nagera, 1966).

CHAPTER 11

Case Illustrations

Adult Cases

Example 1

For methodological reasons I have described in some degree of isolation vicissitudes in the various developmental lines that determine the different oedipal constellations and shape the final form acquired by the sexual organization. In reality a multitude of factors closely interact with one another. The cases that follow are attempts to illustrate *in vivo* many of the points made above, most especially the complexity of the many interacting factors . They will show as well that a correct assessment of the true oedipal constellation of any given patient is only possible through the careful examination of the position reached in each of the five fundamental lines of development and the interactions among them.

Miss K. was twenty-nine years of age at the beginning of the treatment. She had decided to undertake analysis because of her difficulties in her relationships with men. She had had any number of boyfriends and affairs but she invariably started arguments and fights that led to rather dramatic break-ups.

She claimed at the beginning of analysis that there were no suitable men around, that she had no luck, that she had not found the right man for her, etc. Underneath this line of defense she was aware that some fault in her made her consider all men unsuitable for one reason or another.

During her analysis, it became clear that the men she became involved with belonged in one of three very characteristic groups, and that she followed a specific pattern in the choice of her objects. The *first group* consisted of married men with whom she involved herself in a fashion that showed the extent of her unresolved oedipal conflicts. Further, these men tended to be what she described as "damaged" or "poor male specimens." They were not only much older but one of them was an alcoholic, another suffered from epilepsy, etc. Frequently these men had sexual difficulties and were not always potent. Such choice of objects was not accidental, but part of an unconscious campaign to prove to herself that all males were worthless and weak. In this way she tried to control unconscious anxieties, associated with fantasies and unconscious fears that the penis of a really potent male would damage her physically, since she had an anal-sadistic conception of intercourse.

Males of the *second group* were single and younger than the above but similarly "damaged and unsuitable" sexually or well below her social and cultural level. She could look down on them for any of the above reasons.

The *third group* of men she sought out were normal sexually and otherwise, and suitable in terms of education, social group, etc. Her involvement with this type of man was not as frequent as with those of the two previous groups. There is no doubt that this third type of object choice was made by the healthier aspects of her personality. As was to be expected, relationships with this last type of man were the most difficult ones and were short-lived.

For our purposes here we will concentrate on the vicissitudes of her relations with the third group, that of normal men. To start with she was relieved and pleased that a man, single and normal, showed an interest in her, but this was short-lived. It was particularly this group of "normal" men that most strongly aroused her very intense penis envy. She grew more and more restless as she failed to discover in them faults that would prove to her that "they were no better than she was." Her strong penis envy was determined partly by what she considered to be the mother's clear preference and exclusive relation to the males in the family. As a little girl she resented the close relationship that existed between her mother and father, a relationship from which she felt excluded by the mother, for whose company and attention she longed. She was always resentful of the presence of the father and felt very happy whenever the latter had to be away from home. She thought that the mother's preference was based on the fact that the father was "different" (had a penis), a a suspicion that she saw "confirmed" when her brothers were born. Again she was tortured by fantasies of the "special" relation between the mother and her brothers. They too were "different" like the father. For these reasons she envied them intensely and felt aggressive and hostile to them. She had fantasies of her own incompleteness that she contrasted with their completeness. Further, only those who were "complete" were really intelligent and clever intellectually. They were not only prefered by their mothers, but were given every possible advantage in the world only because they had that "thing." She admired them for possessing a penis as much as she hated them. She resented the strong sexual attraction she felt for men and the disappointment she always experienced in spite of this because of her frigidity in sexual intercourse. She was envious of their pleasure, while she had none. Though, as we will see presently, she felt some unconscious attraction toward women, on balance most of her cathexes were directed to males. Consciously her sexual interests and attractions revolved around them in spite of the many sources of interference that will be described.

When she related to a damaged man she was happier, insofar as her penis envy was not so marked with them. As she said, they were living examples showing that men were worthless in spite of their possession of the precious "thing" (6). Indeed, they were no better than she and the whole world was unfair in "discriminating" between her and them. Yet the relationships with this type of man were unhappy and tormented too, since her object choice was based on her contempt for their weaknesses, her envy and hostility. Further, on the basis of a concurrent set of fantasies she demanded that they be "perfect" (they had the

---

6. This was the patient's word for penis. For some time she could not refer to the penis by its name.

penis) and these men were anything but perfect in their achievements, behavior, abilities, sexual capacity, etc.

In her relationship to *normal men*, her penis envy and competitiveness was immediately aroused by their "perfection," especially if they were gifted intellectually. She felt compelled to compete with them in everything, in an attempt to prove that she was at least their equal if not actually more gifted. She argued constantly, even in irrelevant matters, trying to prove her companion wrong. She had an answer for everything and for every problem, political, social, economic, scientific, etc. At the same time she was extremely critical and intolerant of everything her male partners did and voiced her criticism in a hurtful, sadistic manner. She used her knowledge in fields where she was better informed to humiliate them and to assert her superiority. She criticized their driving, their lack of mechanical knowledge (her father had been an outstanding driver and car enthusiast). She always thought she was a better driver and constantly compared herself to them. If in the theater, a restaurant, or even in a bus, she complained that they moved too much in their seats, or sat too stiffly, talked too much or too little, laughed too loudly, embarrassing her, or had no sense of humor, talked too loudly or too softly, were indiscreet, too assertive or too difficult, too sporty or dressed too properly, were too mean in tipping, etc. Further, she took a very active role, usurping many of the male prerogatives, a fact that greatly embarrassed her boyfriends. She resented any of the usual demands males tend to make of their female friends. "Who did they think they were?" she asked.

She hated the idea of being domesticated, washing their shirts, sewing their socks and buttons, etc. At the same time she had underneath it all an equally strong longing for a home, husband, children, in short for the "passive-domesticated" role of a housewife. It was, after all, this wish of a part of her personality that brought her into analysis.

Sexually she was too active and took the initiative frequently, trying to show herself as more experienced and usurping the masculine role. In sexual intercourse she was mostly frigid, and resented having the male on top of her and adopting a passive position. She could occasionally have an orgasm if she took the active role and placed herself on top of her sexual partner. As analysis later demonstrated, she had at such times a fantasy of being the male and possessing the penis herself. This fantasy greatly excited her sexually. Her main source of sexual satisfaction was of an autoerotic nature, through masturbation and the accompanying fantasies, which were mostly barred from consciousness, especially at the beginning of her treatment. Later on, as treatment progressed, her masturbatory sexual fantasies became available, and proved to be mostly of an anal-sadistic nature. They always contained elements of violence and brutality. Women were raped, mistreated, forced, brutally assaulted, damaged, humiliated, etc. Men did not escape unhurt either. There was blood all over the place in many of her fantasies.

At times she took the role of the brutal man assaulting the woman, at others she was the mistreated and assaulted woman. One repressed fantasy, much defended against, that was uncovered in the analysis consisted of pushing into her mother's vagina some red-hot knitting needles. She then realized how much she enjoyed driving her mother to the countryside for an occasional outing as her father had been in the habit of doing in the past. Taking her father's role in this fashion never failed to arouse her to a degree that she started to have full conscious awareness of her sexual excitement. This realization terrified the patient, since she had the strongest possible objections on the ego side to any lesbian tendencies.

Fantasies of violence and torture haunted her much of the time and never failed to arouse her sexually, leading finally to masturbation. Recurring fantasies of this type concerned, for example, the tortures and extermination of the Jews by the Nazis and some very refined old Chinese tortures, especially when applied to men.

In real life she was terrified at the sight of violence and would avoid going to the cinema if a violent picture was being shown. She was terrified of finding any confirmation in actual life of the true existence of the feelings that so excited and frightened her. She had somehow managed to make herself believe that all this violence belonged only in the unreal world of her fantasies and dreams, and was not a part of real life. To find it in reality provoked extreme anxiety, not only because she feared her strong masochistic tendencies and the wish to be mistreated and tortured, but because of the fear that she too might want to act out in real life the content of her sadistic fantasies.

With women she generally had a difficult relationship. She was unconsciously very attracted to young and pretty women and resentful of the fact that these women preferred their male friends to her. She hated men for being able to get closer to them and to possess them. She was afterwards, during the analysis, frequently aware of feeling sexually aroused in the company of some girlfriends but never allowed herself any conscious sexual fantasies about them. They had to be excluded at all cost from conscious awareness. Consciously she dreaded more than anything else "being a lesbian."

If we view this patient in the context of the four lines of development responsible for the final form of her oedipus complex, we can observe the following:

1. *Change of object:* The patient has to some extent changed the object to which her sexual cathexis is directed from the mother to the father. If considered in isolation from the other lines of development, however, this change of object is misleading. Such a change is usually taken to imply that the move from the first to the second stage of the oedipus complex of the girl has been achieved, but we can immediately perceive that such is not the case with the patient. Though it is true that most of her conscious sexual interest and cathexis goes to men, to whom she feels genuinely attracted, *this is not from a passive-feminine,* but an active-masculine position. Precisely because of this all her relationships to normal men were bound to fail, since they were unable to tolerate her after a short while.

2. *The change from the active-masculine to the passive-feminine:* We must note that the patient's masturbatory fantasy life was largely based on her playing a masculine role, and that orgasm during intercourse was only possible if she was able to ride her sexual partner with the fantasy of penetrating him with her phallus.

Indeed the patient was, developmentally speaking, fixated to the first stage of the oedipal phase and *within that first stage her position was that of the inverted complex* (see square [e] of Figure 2, p. 11), where the father has become the essential object of the positive cathexis instead of the mother. I shall discuss some of the reasons for this later on. It is evident that for a woman fully to reach the final *second stage of her oedipal development* there must be not only a change of object (mother to father) but no less important, a change from the active-masculine position to the passive-feminine one, which this patient has been unable to accomplish.

3. *Change in terms of the erotogenic zones:* It is similarly evident from the material that this patient's clitoris always remained her essential erotogenic zone, the vagina playing a small role, if any, beyond that of being the organ to receive the penis.

4. *Degree of ego acceptance of the absence of the penis* (and consequently the degree to which a feminine-passive *identification* had been possible): though in some fantasies the patient imagined herself as having a penis, this was more in line with what she would have wanted than with any real unconscious or conscious belief that she had it, or was to grow one, etc. In other words, though she made use of the fantasy of having a penis at certain points she did not in general deny her lack of it. She had largely accepted this fact and much of her behavior toward the mother, other females, and males, was based on her resentful acceptance of this "inferiority." She had further accepted not only that "she was castrated" but similarly that all women were without a penis. The fantasy that there exist some women with a phallus played no special role in her fantasy life, but was only a vestige or residue of that phase of development in children where this belief is universal. For her, males were the privileged ones and on this fact was based much of her penis envy and resentment toward the masculine sex. As earlier stated, an ego acceptance of these facts even with a concomitant revolt against them, is a necessary precondition for a normal move into the second stage of the oedipus complex in girls. Yet, the reverse does not hold true; accepting the absence of the penis is in itself no guarantee that the move will take place, in the absence of other necessary factors. The patient had accepted reality, though under strong

protest, and without abandoning the active-masculine stance. It is certainly more difficult to take the step to femininity (during treatment or even developmentally) if the ego clings to the unconscious fantasy of being a male. Presumably the extension to the vagina from the clitoris as an essential part of the final erotogenic zone for the female exercises an analogous favorable or unfavorable influence. I believe that this ego acceptance is a positive prognosis for treatment, especially so in comparison with those patients where the ego clings to a belief in its masculinity, thus adding another problem to be resolved.

In the patient under discussion a multiplicity of factors contributed to the interference with a fuller and healthier identification with the passive-feminine aspects of the mother, and to my mind, explain this patient refusal to abandon the active-masculine position, in spite of the fact that her ego had fully accepted her lack of a penis.

To start with, the mother was by far the dominant figure in the household, being herself rather masculine and active and consequently not an appropriate figure for a passive-feminine identification. The father was rather withdrawn from the children, and preferred to absorb himself in the different businesses of the family. He consequently did not welcome and was not sufficiently receptive to the overtures of the little girl. Furthermore, even at a conscious level the father at times resented the existence of the children who, according to him, monopolized the attention of his wife, and spoke of this in front of his children. While this patient was at the peak of her positive active-masculine attachment to the mother, her first sibling was born—a common enough event that had important repercussions. The girl reacted to it by clinging further to the mother from her active-masculine position and not, as is frequently the case, with the intense disappointment that turns the little girl toward the father that gives the babies, and away from the mother who has "betrayed" them. This consolidation of the active-masculine position was in turn determined by a number of other reasons. The patient had an important anal-sadistic fixation and conceived of childbirth and intercourse as a painful, brutal, hurting and damaging experience. The strong masochistic (and sadistic) elements in her personality precluded a feminine identification that, according to her fantasies would lay her open to the savage attacks of men and the dangers and pains of childbirth. We can remark here on the importance of the qualitative aspects of these processes. Some masochism (feminine masochism) is favorable to the necessary passive-feminine identification while too much, as in the present case, can constitute a serious obstacle to such an identification. The strength of the patient's sado-masochistic makeup and fantasies and of her anal-sadistic fixations were in part due to the severity of her toilet-training experience. Thus, the mother and the maternal grandmother quite frequently and forcefully administered enemas to the child, who violently objected to them. Beyond this, during her earlier years she was constantly bombarded by accounts of the tortures and extermination of Jewish people by the Nazis. This included stories of experiments where women were forced to give birth with their legs tied together (7). The patient also received, too early, too much information about sex and childbirth, for instance through gynecological medical textbooks illustrating the different stages of childbirth, etc. Naturally enough, far from enlightening, this excessive information at an early age frightened her, triggering off many terrifying fantasies about sex, childbirth, etc. All the above factors combined to make a passive-feminine identification a near impossibility. Clearly, the safest position in the circumstances was to remain a "castrated male."

To summarize, the patient changed the object mother for the object father without abandoning the active-masculine position of the first stage of the oedipus complex in girls; the clitoris remained the essential erotogenic zone and from the ego point of view she accepted the lack of a penis in herself and other females, under protest, but was not able to achieve a complete and healthy passive-feminine identification with the mother.

The patient's fundamental oedipal position thus places her in the first stage of the oedipus complex with an "inverted complex." Though the description of the point around which she has essentially organized her oedipal complex is accurate, there were some

---

7. The patient's mother was Jewish and very narrowly escaped with some other relatives the Nazis' persecution in Holland.

partial, tentative moves of small portions of her drive organization into various other directions, just as some of it remained attached to the object mother. As evidence of the latter there are the fantasies of possessing the mother (sexually and otherwise) and as evidence of the former there is the strong wish to become a "domesticated" housewife, to have children and to care for and admire without ambivalence and envy her husband to be. There were, too, a few occasions, especially during adolescence, when she felt that the mother was not a good wife to the father and when she wished her away in order to care for him as a good wife would. At that time she was able to admire him for his kindness and professional and business accomplishments. This move into the second stage was limited in the amount of libido reaching it and there seems to have been a quick withdrawal from that position.

With the further progress of treatment and the analysis of her excessive masochism and anal sadism, her penis envy and its sources, she was able to accept a passive-feminine role in her relationship to men. Soon afterwards the patient made a suitable marriage, became pregnant and had her first child.

Example 2

Miss Q. was an attractive young secretary, twenty-four years of age and single. She came to treatment because of difficulties with her family and in her social relationships, as well as a number of other incapacitating symptoms to be described below. The difficulties with her family had been long-standing: she and her father had not spoken to each other since she had left the household several years before. There were difficulties, too, with her mother and a younger sister, Z.

The patient had come from a modest, working-class background of which she was very ashamed. She was ambitious socially, educated herself through reading and managed to become an efficient secretary instead of going into factory work, as would have been likely with her background. Being attractive, well mannered and well spoken (she made enormous efforts to speak good English without a trace of the accent that was typical of her family and social group) she was now moving in what she considered a higher social class, of professional people and their friends. She was proud of this and was determined to marry someone of this professional group. This ambition and the fact that she avoided her own social group, family, friends, etc., was a constant source of difficulty with her family. They felt she despised them; this she conveyed quite openly, feeling guilty afterwards. They complained that they were not good enough for her, etc.

Yet when with her new friends on social occasions such as parties, dinners, etc., the patient was symptomatic. She was anxious for days before any such event, she felt sick (butterflies in her stomach) and frequently ended up vomiting. Thus, for example, at a dinner party she would be terrified, with an uneasy feeling that she did not belong there; the sick feeling would develop and she would finally feel forced to leave the table and vomit. After that, she would return to the dinner table, or on occasion she had to leave the party altogether because of the level of her remaining anxiety. The intensity and frequency of these symptoms had so increased that at the point of initiating treatment she had developed a social inhibition, avoiding most invitations. Further, though she had recovered most of her weight by the beginning of the treatment, she had previously lost about fifteen pounds, apparently because of these symptoms.

Finally, she had difficulties in her working relationships and had been changing jobs with increasing frequency.

At the time of beginning treatment she had been living away from home for several years but visited on occasion. Such visits always ended badly, with bitter arguments and accusations. The family criticized her "high airs," the way she dressed (elegantly) and especially the fact that she never brought any of her friends or boyfriends home.

She remembered her childhood as miserable, especially after a hospitalization when she was three years of age. At that time, though she had been toilet-trained since the age of ten months, she regressed to bedwetting, a symptom that persisted until her early teens. She was in the hospital (in quarantine) for a period of about three months suffering from scarlet fever and several complications. This had been a traumatic experience for her.

Her sister, Z., was born when the patient was about six years old. She remembers very badly wanting a sibling since she felt lonely and yet being very miserable after that time, for several reasons. Her sister, according to the patient, was a very pretty blue-eyed baby that delighted parents, family and friends. Presents and attention were showered on the baby while she felt suddenly totally neglected. The sister grew into a cute, pretty girl and later into a very attractive adolescent that everybody admired and praised while she felt sad, bitter, and ignored. To complicate matters further, the mother became very depressed after the birth of Z. with a postpartum depression that persisted for the next three years. Since the mother was so incapacitated she was forced at this tender age and up to the age of eight or nine to take a good portion of the care of her sister and of the family generally.

At five she started school and remembers dreading going and being terrified while there. Shortly after starting school one of her peers, another girl, died in school after a fall on the stairs; she felt this might have contributed further to the difficult time she was having adapting to it.

As she remembered it, the economic situation at home was very difficult in those days. Her mother was very sensitive about not having money and it was important to her not to let other people know about their difficulties. Bitterly, the patient remarked that it was the mother who put grandiose ideas into her head.

The parents' marriage was generally stormy. They argued constantly, the father accusing the mother of being unfaithful, especially after the mother took a job in a tavern. The patient was then around ten years of age, but it seems that similar situations had existed from much earlier in the patient's life.

She claimed that she hated her father now and that she was full of hostile feelings toward him, while her relationship to her mother was better. Yet she vaguely remembered that as a little girl she had tried very hard to please her father and was always on his side whenever there were arguments between her parents.

The material that follows was selected as a further illustration of the subject matter under discussion. It is presented as it unfolded chronologically during a period of approximately a year and a half. The sequence in which the material is presented is exactly the order in which it appeared during the course of her treatment sessions, though on occasion the vignettes presented may have followed one another in consecutive sessions, while at other times a gap of a week or more may exist between them.

The selection of the material is biased in the direction of illustrating the complexities of the oedipus complex of any given patient. Other meanings, determinants, and possible interpretations of the material have been excluded purposely so as not to obscure unnecessarily the central issue.

A very sensitive area for this patient was what she referred to as her lack of education. Early in her analysis she had devoted much time to this. Once, after several months of treatment, a girlfriend asked the patient about her education. This, as was usually so, greatly upset Miss Q. She felt bad, blushed deep red, felt embarrassed and anxious. She lied, saying that she had gone to academy X (a distinguished school for secretaries) during the day and had done very well, while in fact, she had had to work during the day in order to finance study at a not very reputable place during the evenings. At this point, the patient was very upset and bitterly complained about her parents, who were unable to give her a "proper" education. She felt at an enormous disadvantage compared with other people. She was convinced that everything would be different for her if she had a "proper" education, asking the therapist, "Don't you think so too?"

I reminded her that, as on other occasions in the past, she was expressing in a symbolic displaced manner the fact that she was born a girl and not a boy. The "missing part" that is, the "proper education," being a reference to the absent penis.

Given my knowledge of the patient and her family background I venture the reconstruction that it was likely that her parents had wanted a boy as their first child. They were disappointed that instead, she, a girl had been born. I added that this might have stimulated in her the wish to be a boy. Perhaps she could understand now what she really meant when she complained of how different things would have been for her had she had a "proper" education.

She recalled with much affect that indeed that was so. Her parents, both of them, had wanted a boy. In fact, her mother had told her so specifically. Mother had further stated many times that she really liked boys, not girls, and in that sense the patient and her sister were a disappointment for her. She remembered when little boys (cousins) visited her home and how much attention they received from her parents. Her mother simply adored them, while she felt jealous that such a fuss was made of the little boys.

As further confirmation she mentioned that her father took her to all sorts of events and activities that were proper for a boy, not a girl. She remembered, with much feeling and tears, her wishing very strongly at that time that she be a boy. She refused, as she recalled, to play with girls or at girlish things. She was always with the boys and behaved like one of them all the time. She could understand now too why she had been a tomboy for so long. She added that that was what she means nowadays when she mentions fantasies that she could not tell me. She could not even really describe them well to herself, but they were "of a male character," of "male intensity." "I do not mean having feelings for other females, but nevertheless something that is wrong."

After this session the patient was more able to see the highly symbolic meaning of much of her behavior and symptoms, for example, why she considered herself a "fake." She pretended to be something she was not, i.e., educated; from a good, educated, middle-class family; with some manners and speech accents that were not those of either her family or her social group, etc. Much of this behavior could be partly understood as different ways in which she "pretended" to be different from what she really was, that is, a boy instead of a girl. Indeed, in her social group, if anybody had a chance to be educated it would be the boys, because girls had no right to such ambitions. Her father frequently stated this as a response to the patient's wishes in this regard and actually refused financing any of her minimal expenses beyond the elementary school grades.

We discovered too that she had an inordinate fear of being examined by a gynecologist. She postponed a visit to him for quite a while in spite of rather mortifying symptoms until she understood from her analysis her fear of "being found out."

The same applied partly to her fear of social events, gatherings, dinners, etc. Here too, invariably one of her fears was that she would be found out for "what she was."

Shortly afterwards she mentioned, for the first time, that her father was always complaining about his tummy when she was a child. I remarked on the similarity of her symptoms to those of her father and the "being like father" (identification) quality of it. Much to my surprise she was astonished at the similarity, remembering then how actually as a child and to this day she had a wish to look physically as her father, whose physique she greatly admired.

A few days later she and her boyfriend were to go to a party. She had her usual anxiety and apprehensions, only that a new twist was added. At the party most of the girls would be models, attractive and very pretty. Again, she felt that she would be at a disadvantage, in reality without reason since the patient was herself an attractive young woman. Her own roommate, A. (a model) was going to be there too. When the time came she "found herself transformed." She had not been anxious at all, in fact she enjoyed herself enormously. After the party she had petted with her boyfriend and felt very aroused. She wanted her boyfriend to make love to her, but much to her disappointment, he could not perform. After he left she was angry and in tears. She felt anxious, restless, and could not fall asleep. She was haunted by painful and distressing thoughts that her boyfriend was not attracted to her since he could not perform sexually. She thought that he was attracted to her roommate (A., the model), and though she had no reason whatsoever to think this way, she could not remove the thought from her mind. I reminded the patient that she had told me frequently in the past how attractive she thought A. was. Now she was attributing these thoughts and attractions to her boyfriend. Further, she had moved with A. to a new apartment at A.'s request—an inconvenient move for her, made in order to stay with A. I reminded her how angry, disappointed, and jealous she had felt, shortly after the move, when A. commented that maybe the patient would have to move out since she (A.) was considering marriage.

I suggested that maybe she was more attracted "sexually" to A.

than she could acknowledge, an interpretation that she had always refused. This time the patient said, "That is true," and remembered clearly how at the party she felt hypnotized by A.'s beauty. She could not take her eyes from her during the whole party and especially from her bust. "A. is so beautiful, especially there, in contrast to me." She added that she remembered other occasions when she had been attracted sexually to other women, especially to their busts if they were of substantial proportions. Her mother, her sister, and she had small busts. Nowadays this was a disappointment to her. Her present boyfriend liked large busts too, and that upset her since she felt she was not "as well endowed as she ought to be." This dissatisfaction was partly seen to be a displacement upwards of her dissatisfaction with her genitals, especially the absence of the penis. Further, being "plain" there sort of confirmed that she was like a boy. So far as she had a strong wish to be feminine, she felt discouraged at the lack of this feminine attribute.

As a follow-up to the party, her roommate A. referred to the patient's boyfriend as somebody nice and clever. Some of the other models liked him, too. She reacted with anger, dismay, and jealousy. The latter in the sense that all these attractive girls reacted in positive terms to him and clearly had liked him more than her. Dejected, she "acknowledged" to herself the fact that the boyfriend was stronger, had more education, more personality, etc. She could easily see her envy of him as a boy. He had "more personality," "more education," etc. Everybody did prefer boys to girls anyhow (like her parents).

The recognition of her interest in all these model girls, of her wish that she be more admired and more attractive to them than her boyfriend made her frightened. It stirred up all of her homosexual longings and anxieties that she had so far managed to deny and dispose of. She was concerned that the recognition of such impulses and the recovery of memories, fantasies, etc., of this type endangered her. She thought that maybe she would act on them and yet she did not want to be a homosexual at all.

As the days went by there were more fantasies about her attractive roommate A. They *generally followed* those occasions when she had been aroused sexually by her boyfriend and yet could not be satisfied by him because of his impotency. It became clear to her that in such a state she would like to have A. release her of her sexual tension. "She has such a nice bust and is so beautiful." The patient understood her masculine identification and especially verbalized her anger at the "passive role" she was forced into by being a girl. She had to wait for somebody to approach her to get her sexual satisfaction while boys could go after girls whenever they felt like it. She felt now strongly that she wanted to be a boy so as not to be dependent on somebody else sexually. That way, she said, she could be active and satisfy herself, for example, with A.

She referred a few days later, amidst much distress and guilt while mentioning it, to how her boyfriend had wanted to have relations with her through her back passage. It had been very painful for her. Yet she had been astonished because he had a "tremendous erection and orgasm." "By the front he always loses his erection or has a very weak one," she added. She was worried about him because she thought this must be something homosexual, as with her own fantasies. She wanted to help him with his sexual problems, but if he preferred that way to the other way she would have no pleasure. She would ask repeatedly: Did I think it was wrong to do that? Her boyfriend told her that he could not control this wish and that he was always thinking of having her this way. He told her too of an incident as a child that still terrified him. He had become excited and had had an erection by "skin contact" with another male (8). She reacted to this with fear, thinking that if he could not control himself (his homosexual tendencies, as she thought) maybe she would not be able to either.

I had the distinct impression, that as on other occasions. I had not yet heard the full story about this experience of anal intercourse. Frequently, when talking about difficult subjects, the patient would introduce them in a roundabout way. First the account was distorted, biased, as if she were testing the ground, until finally she was able to relate the full version of the event.

---

8. The patient's boyfriend was in psychotherapy too and they occasionally exchanged such confidences.

By her manner, excitement, questions, it was clear that she had enjoyed the experience very much, including the pain she had experienced. It was clear, too, that somewhere she felt low, dirty, mistreated, etc. Yet all of these feelings seemed to have contributed in some way to her enjoyment of the experience.

When I pointed out that there was more to this episode than the pain and the concerns she had expressed so far, she acknowledged that she had herself been very interested in anal intercourse. She had in fact seduced and encouraged him to do so. She admitted that the whole thing had been very exciting for her: She was delighted to see him so very much potent and excited.

Much later on in her treatment, this and other similar experiences could be understood in the context of another unconscious fantasy, of which she had had occasional glimpses. She was not a girl but a castrated boy. Since she could not possess the girls that she wanted because of the absence of a penis, she, as a boy, had no alternative but to have a man penetrate him (her) anally. Further, as we will see, the experience was the re-enactment of early primal scene observations that she had interpreted as anal intercourse. In this sense she was identifying with the mother who was violated by father from behind.

At a later date in her treatment it happened that her menstruation had been delayed for a few days. Though there was no reason to assume she could be pregnant, since appropriate precautions had been taken, she was terrified at the conscious level that that might be the case. Unconsciously she badly wanted to have a baby, a wish that seemed to go back to at least her adolescence and late latency. She remembered how much she had wanted to give her father a baby boy. She was never conscious of giving it to him herself, but by other various means. Yet she was conscious of hating her mother who at the time was working at a tavern, a fact her father disliked. As a result there were arguments at home between the parents with the father accusing the mother of running around with other men and threatening divorce. It was then that the patient had fantasies of going away with her father, leaving mother behind. She would look after him and make him happy. She thought she understood him much better than mother did and that in some ill-defined form she would give him a son.

In this way father would love her very much and there would be the three of them only, father, she and the son that she felt father longed for so very much.

Around this time she finally managed to take her boyfriend home to meet her parents. She was terrified that he would not like them. In fact, he liked them very much and, contrary to her expectations, her parents were very friendly to the boyfriend, particularly her father. She was pleased by this yet at the same time was very upset with her father, whom she clearly expected to be jealous and argue or fight with the boyfriend. Further, the boyfriend had been critical of her, of the way she talked down to her parents, of her cold manner toward them. She was devastated by these criticisms, adding that she hated her father with a passion. She could kill him. He should be dead. He should have been shot years ago. He should be run over by an underground train (where he actually worked). Why didn't her mother leave him? He ruined everybody's life, etc. No sooner had she mentioned that mother ought to leave him that a thought went like a flash through her mind. He would then be really sad and she could go then and look after him! She felt upset at this thought because she was very fond of her mother, yet was unable to show it. At times she would like to put an arm around her, kiss her or touch her in some way. She knew the mother would welcome this, but she could never do it. She concluded that it was probably related to the undemonstrative way they had been raised. I pointed out that there might be other reasons that a girl might avoid physical contact with her mother. She quickly picked up the homosexual threat, agreeing that it must be something like that since it was so irrational on her part.

There were more visits with her boyfriend at home, with very similar results. The boyfriend particularly criticized her for her behavior toward her mother, the patient's air of superiority toward her, etc. Again, she was devastated, crying bitterly as she remembered some childhood material she had connected with the boyfriend's criticisms. Her father used to defend the mother and would play one against the other. When he was angry with mother and accusing her of all sorts of things he would come to her and tell her how nasty the mother was. He would ask her not to talk to her mother any more, saying he would divorce her and he and the patient would live together without the mother. Though such talk frightened her, she was pleased and excited by it. Yet her father always let her down because soon afterwards he would be on good terms with the mother again and then would turn against her. She could see clearly why she was so much affected by the boyfriend's criticism. He too was saying that mother was right, and nice, while she was nasty and wrong. She added that she simply could not take it and would break with the boyfriend. She needed support, not criticism.

Around this time she recalled too how it was that her love and admiration for her father turned into an incredible hate. She said, "I turned against him like a vicious dog." She was thirteen years old at the time and had been doing well at school. For that reason she could go to another good school to continue her education. Father refused this, saying to her that he had supported her long enough and now she had to repay him. She remembered thinking then that if she could study she could give him a lot of money. Nevertheless, she so wanted to please him that she got a job where she earned about $22.00 a week. When she came home willing to give her father half her earnings, he demanded it all except for one dollar. She was so angry, she said, because she "realized" that he did not really love or care for her. "He gambled you know and drank," she said sobbing, and "I realized that even his gambling and drinking were more important to him than I was."

From there onwards she turned "vicious" toward him. Interestingly enough, she had to some extent recreated this situation in the present with the boyfriend. She had at her insistence lent him money which he did not in reality need, since he earned well. She on the other hand really needed all the pennies she could put together. She could understand now, too, why she was always demanding things from the boyfriend. She considered any occasion whatsoever an appropriate time for a present, or for a special treat, etc. If the boyfriend failed to do so she became enraged with him and accused him of not caring for her, of using her for his own purposes, etc. She had to be reassured that he was not like the father. On the other hand, since she expected presents on rather unusual, untraditional occasions, she created the stage for disappointment.

It soon became clear that her disappointment when father had met the boyfriend (and gotten along very well with him) was related to her fantasy that she would show father what she could get for herself. Father had wanted her to be modest and only to go out with working-class people like themselves. The boyfriend was educated, indeed, a professional man. She was saying to her father: you may not care for me but look whom I got. He is so much better than you are (9).

The above associations reminded her of another boyfriend she had had earlier, a wealthy boy for whom she was quite ostentatiously knitting a sweater, with the conscious hope of irritating and making her father jealous. This she achieved, since the father finally exploded in a rage, saying that she never did anything like that for him.

As this material unfolded in the sessions, her behavior at the office with her employer, Mr. K., an older professional man, became very seductive. This had indeed happened many times in the past as part of the compulsion to repeat and act out some of her unconscious conflicts. She said that she found Mr. K. attractive and desirable, in spite of his age. She was turned on sexually by him and had any number of fantasies of going out with him and how this would come to pass. She wanted him to embrace her and kiss her passionately. She wanted to know how his mouth felt. She commented that she should not be thinking like that since she was engaged. When I said that thinking did nobody much damage, by itself, implying that there is a difference between thinking and doing, she said, "Well, it's not only thinking, you know, I actually would like it to happen."

Her seductiveness, which was quite active, did not go unnoticed by Mr. K. She said to him that it was a pity that the glasses he wore did not favor him, since he was such an attractive man. Mr. K. took the cue and introduced a sexual subject into their conversation. On this occasion, thanks to the insights she

---

9. At still another level she was offering the father the son he had always wanted.

had been acquiring, she was able to stop her acting out short. In the past, she would have proceeded further, seduced her boss, and acquired irrational expectations about the relationship—that he would divorce his wife and marry her, etc. As this failed to happen she would become angry, and would finally be fired or would leave in a huff on her own.

At times she could be quite cruel and devastating in her comments to males, yet more frequently than not this was a reaction to feeling unwanted, unloved, and rejected by them. For example, on one occasion, she had a bad cold and was very upset that the boyfriend had not visited her the night before. "If he really cared for me, he would have come." The boyfriend phoned her the following morning at work and told her quite nicely to take care of her cold. He added that she should keep warm in bed that evening. She retorted acrimoniously that she was intending to look for an attractive young man to keep her warm that evening. The boyfriend did not like this, she thought, but did not say anything about it except that he was glad that she did not work at his office, the implication being that he would be so excited all the time that he would not be able to do any work. In a rather nasty tone, she retorted that she doubted it, because she thought that neither she nor any other girl would really be able to warm him up. He was very hurt by this clear and derisive allusion to his sexual difficulties. She knew this was cruel but felt so hurt that he had not come to see her the evening before that she felt compelled to pay him back. The harking back to her disappointment in the father, mentioned before, was an important determinant of her behavior. As she said, when in this mood she could be vicious.

As time went by she understood better the overwhelming anxiety she felt at times that all other women were more attractive than she was, although she knew that that was not really so. Worse still, she would panic at the thought that any girl could take away from her whatever boyfriend she had. She understood the conflict in which her femininity was caught. She longed to be a boy because both parents wanted a boy. Her overtures to her father as a girl ended in disaster, as she saw it, and she felt ill-equipped since she thought her bust to be small. In reality, she was quite attractive and her bust looked quite satisfactory.

She recovered innumerable memories from her childhood, where she saw herself as a failure because she could not arouse her father's interest. She remembered how in competing with mother for the father's attention, the mother always had had the upper hand. Particularly painful were those memories, already referred to, where father would be angry with mother and come close to her, only to let her down shortly afterwards. She could connect this with her present irrational fear that all other women were so much more attractive than she and that her boyfriends would think so too, and leave her for any one of them. She added that in some cases, as with S. (a girlfriend), she knew very well that she (the patient) was much more attractive, yet still felt that way.

The question of her being promiscuous worried her. She mentioned how an old boyfriend of hers had phoned and that she decided to go to his apartment right then and there. She explained her action as a result of discouragement with her present boyfriend who, though talking about marriage, was essentially avoiding the issue. She felt he was playing with her in this regard, and she longed for a family and for children. Further, she felt frustrated sexually since he was frequently impotent. More than that, she had to prove to herself that she was attractive as a female, that other males would get excited with her. Otherwise she felt terrible. Her present boyfriend only increased her insecurities about her worth, her looks, and her sexual desirability to men. In any case, as soon as she arrived at L.'s apartment, he started fondling her. That pleased her because he looked very excited and she found that reassuring. L. had asked her to take off her shoes, he did the same, and they danced all night. He had put the lights off and brought some candles. It all looked very romantic.

She explained that though they had had a closer relationship in the past, he had never pressed her for intercourse. He had been content with mutual masturbation. He did not this time, either, which infuriated her. She asked him about this and he explained to her that he did not want to have intercourse until he married. She did not believe that and told him that there was something wrong with him and he ought to have psychoanalysis. He was very embarrassed but she felt quite relaxed talking to him about sex. She was pleased that "she was in command" and he was embarrassed, and though disappointed that he would not have intercourse, she could dismiss it as his problem. It was obvious to her how sexually aroused he had been with her, though frightened of intercourse. At this point, she asked if I had read *Nana*, Zola's novel.

She explained that Nana was a prostitute who seduced a very rich and distinguished count, a very pious man who had married a frigid woman thought to be very pious too; in fact, she had many lovers. The count simply went mad about Nana, he could not resist her. The patient admired this woman very much—"She is very kind, you know, though she is a prostitute"—adding that she had many fantasies of being a prostitute herself. She supposed that she felt disappointed that she was unable to seduce L. to have intercourse.

Her associations led to her father's accusing her mother of running around with many men, of being a prostitute. He also accused the patient of this. "You see, shortly after I was thirteen, when he wanted all my money, I became very interested in boys, dated a lot of different boys, came home late, etc. I think I did it to irritate him, to make him jealous but he accused me too, of running around, of being a prostitute, like my mother." With much affect she added, "He even threw me out of the house."

Several things became clear, including the fact that she had many prostitution and promiscuity fantasies that she found highly stimulating and at the same time very, very frightening. She was horrified that she would not have any control over her sexual impulses and fantasies and that she would be at their mercy, acting them out, something that only occasionally happened. In fact, what she most wanted was to find a nice man that would love her, marry her, and give her a family. She wanted to be, in her words, "a domesticated housewife." Yet as we have seen, there were so many unconscious and conscious conflictual situations that interfered with this ideal that she was not quite likely to realize it. In fact, her relationships with males were difficult, tormenting, disappointing and tending to end badly for her since they were in great part overridden by her childhood fantasies, longings, and conflicts.

Further, we could conclude that most of her various stable boyfriends through the years had been well chosen. They had had "morals" and did not approve of sex before marriage or were essentially impotent, at least to start with, as was her present boyfriend. This situation made her feel safe and in control, not only of her sexual impulses but of those of her sexual partners. On the rare occasions when she found a "normal" male she quickly put distance between them, out of the fear that she might have been in his power sexually. In other words, she feared that they would so excite her that she might not be able to control herself and be forced to do "things" that she disapproved of.

When such fantasies came into the transference and she wanted to play Nana the prostitute with her analyst, we could ascertain not only the strength of her sexual wishes but her fear of losing control, of prostituting herself, of being able to seduce the analyst and other males. She referred with much visible anxiety to her fear of ending like Nana. In the novel, she explained, Nana manages to corrupt everything she touches. The whole thing ends in disaster, one of the characters dies of smallpox, the other is shot. Sobbing, she added, that "they were all ruined economically and morally."

Her innumerable fantasies about the older men that she worked for were clearly linked to her unresolved oedipal longings. In this context, she recalled how, when she was thirteen years old, she saw her parents having intercourse. Not only that, she heard what they were saying to each other. She explained that they had some guests at home at the time who were occupying the parental bedroom. A bed had been placed in her room where the parents were sleeping temporarily. It was late, father came home and, assuming that the patient was sleeping, started to fondle the mother. Mother was reluctant because of the presence of the patient. Father said he had been very excited by some young, pretty girls he had seen at work and on the way home. The mother answered, somewhat irritated but simultaneously excited, "You should have gone with them," to which the father retorted that he had waited to come home to her. She remembered being very excited sexually and feeling guilty that she was witnessing all of this. She understood how in her fantasies about older men she saw herself as one of the young, pretty girls that father was excited about.

Her masturbation fantasies, though variable, were variations on a consistent theme. She was a prostitute rendering her services to various "faceless" men. They were hardly ever identifiable, she claimed, at this point in her treatment.

She remembered that at about the age of thirteen or thereabouts she developed a tremendous curiosity about prostitutes. She read everything she was able to get her hands on at the library. She had an uncle who gave her a lot of pornographic literature that she read with great pleasure. As far as she remembers, he (the uncle) never made any advances towards her but there was a cousin of hers that said that he actually did. In any case, she clearly recalled wishing him to do so and being disappointed. In fact, in those days she had many fantasies of prostituting herself with the different males of the family.

It should be remembered that it was at thirteen that she turned "viciously" against her father and her interest in prostitution seems to have started about then. Many months later in her treatment, we were to discover that her turning against father had followed after her witnessing the parents having intercourse, and overhearing their interaction. At this time she referred again to the incident, adding some very illuminating details that I shall describe below. Finally, the primal scene she witnessed came during a period when mother and father were at loggerheads, and in fact talking about divorce. She remembered being angry with mother, thinking that she did not understand father and that she was unfaithful to him. In her fantasy, on this occasion the parents' rift was final and she would go to live with her father and be able to look after him properly. She had been very actively learning to cook the type of food she knew her father liked particularly well, as a preparation for when she would be looking after him.

When the vacation came, she went away with her boyfriend and very much enjoyed playing the role of a good wife to him, being passive with him, trying to please him in everything. Yet this enjoyment was disturbed when the boyfriend forced her to pay for some of her expenses, including one occasion when he forced her to buy her own ice cream. She felt that he did not care, he was like father, he really did not like her or she was not attractive enough to him. She was being treated like a friend, not like a woman that one is attracted to and loves. This thought would upset her greatly and after these incidents she would become harsh and mean, hating the fact that she had tried to please him and had behaved in a "submissive" manner to him.

She could see the obvious associations and similarities to her reactions to her father early in her life. Yet that knowledge did not help to make these incidents any less painful.

She elaborated that incidents of that type had occcurred before. Some years before she had gone on vacation with a different boy-friend and had reacted in much the same way. She was pleased when he bought for her whatever she wanted, especially ice cream, cookies, etc. When it was pointed out that this sounded more like the reaction of a little girl to her father or mother than the relationship between two adults, she remembered the following fantasy. Just before coming to her analysis, when she was feeling so very ill, she used to day-dream a lot that her father was very wealthy and generous toward her. In one of these fantasies she saw herself going to a shop to buy clothes for a vacation she was to take with her parents. Friends asked her where she got all that money to buy clothes. She then answered, delighted, "Oh, it's a present from daddy."

She remembered, too, that father used to bring presents frequently for her much younger sister. She felt jealous and angry but when she protested about this, her father would say, you are too old for presents and she is little. You had yours when you were younger and there is not enough money for presents for both of you anyhow.

Nowadays, she wanted to turn boyfriends into generous fathers who would never refuse her anything. Since she was unusually and rather childishly demanding this frequently led to difficulties. The boyfriends felt exploited and the patient was irrationally angry and gave maladaptive responses to the bemused boyfriends.

Around this time several of her friends, who had been married in the previous year or so, were starting to have babies. She became very depressed since she so wanted to have children herself and to be married. She was growing more and more uncertain that her boyfriend meant to marry her. As a reaction, she bought several dresses for herself and developed fantasies that you could have babies without being married. She became more militant in actively trying to seduce her boss, as well as being very seductive during her sessions. If nobody wanted to marry her, surely somebody would at least find her attractive enough for intercourse. That way she would have her babies at least.

After the patient had been in treatment for a year she was suddenly struck by the many similarities between her present boyfriend and her father. According to her, physically and in character there was a striking resemblance between them. She was astonished that up to this point, although she had had some awareness of this, she had avoided fully acknowledging the fact. She thought that perhaps this explained the way her present illness and disturbing symptoms had actually started.

She had taken a new job. Her present boyfriend, whom she had not yet met, worked there on the professional staff. The first time she saw him she felt "as if struck by lightning" and felt ill immediately, having to leave the room in order to vomit. It was the first time this and other symptoms appeared. She claimed not to be aware at that point of the striking resemblance of this man to her father. Nevertheless, she felt very aroused sexually by him and decided on the spot that was the man she wanted.

As we have seen she indeed managed to obtain him, and during the development of their relationship became more and more symptomatic and disturbed, until she was finally referred for treatment.

The above account was followed by memories dating from when she was twelve years of age. She recalled another girl telling her of a mutual friend who was having intercourse with her father. She was not horrified (though the girl telling the story was), and in fact she thinks she welcomed being told because she used to day-dream about that possibility. She had numerous fantasies, even recently, of her father doing something to her sexually. Yet she remembers one occasion when she was taking a bath upstairs and heard her father coming up the stairs. She hurried to lock the door, which she had not done before, fearful and certain that father was coming up to force her to have sexual intercourse with him. She stated that for several years she was really very frightened whenever she was left alone with him. She can see now how she had transformed her wish into a fear and how she had been blaming the father for her own "perverted" wishes, as she would describe them. She could understand, too, why she forced situations that led to her move away from home, her desire to be on bad terms with him, and many of her general attitudes toward him: she had to put some distance between him and her wishes.

In one of the sessions that followed, she referred to a very satisfactory experience of intercourse with the boyfriend, during which she had reached a climax. Interestingly, she added, at a certain point in the foreplay, she thought about the connections we had been making in her sessions between her father and the boyfriend. She felt frightened and went cold. It took some effort on her part to forget about it and to start kissing and cuddling the boyfriend again, until she had intercourse and an orgasm.

Shortly after this, and while material similar to that I have been discussing was being analyzed, the patient decided to restore the relationship with her father. It had been years since they had talked to each other and she was frightened of his possible reaction. She started visiting home more frequently. Once she bought a present for her father on his birthday but was afraid to give it to him. She gave it to her mother, who passed it on to him. It seemed as if both she and father were uncertain about how to become friends again. Further, the patient would have liked to move back home; in her economic circumstances this would have been very sensible, but she did not dare.

She went home for the next weekend but on Sunday she felt ill all day. "You know, like vomiting but without doing so," she said. When I wondered what had been wrong, she connected it with a present, a hair dryer, she had received from the father. He did not give it to her directly but through her mother. It only made things difficult for her. At first she thought, well, this was an opportunity to talk to him, but she could not bring herself to do it. "By the evening, father was in a bad mood, arguing with mother and I was so frightened that I left the house without even saying thank you." Her boyfriend was appalled at her behavior and she promised him that with his moral support she would talk to her father sometime during the week.

She reported a dream in which a male was trying to force her to submit to him. Her shoulders and head were lying down in a chair while the man was holding her by the waist so that her legs were wide apart as if they were about to have intercourse. Both were naked and she suddenly realized (in the dream) that in fact they were performing for an audience. She was very excited sexually during the dream and woke up disappointed, thinking "such an intense feeling, and it's not going to happen."

Her associations went in the direction that her boyfriend was forcing her to submit and have intercourse when she really did not want to. Although this aspect of her psychopathology will not be discussed in detail, it was clear that she had encouraged or provoked him into this behavior and was now alarmed by it. To the position she had adopted in the dream, she associated another occasion when she witnessed the primal scene. This was several months before the occasion already described. She said that her parents had gone into their bedroom at 2 P.M., leaving her alone in the living room. She thought this odd and after a while walked into the parents' bedroom, without knocking on the door, and saw them having intercourse in a position similar to the one in the dream. Father was holding mother by the waist and mother was being penetrated from behind while reclining on the bed or on something else. The patient turned on her heels and was later told by the mother to knock on the door before walking into the room in the future.

Her associations led to the boyfriend with whom she had had intercourse for the first time. She remembered that they had agreed to have intercourse primarily because she had actively insisted that the boyfriend do it. He was hesitant, thinking it was wrong and they should not do this before marriage. She remembered that when they finally had intercourse she had been thinking of this scene between her parents. She had been disappointed because the boyfriend was inexperienced (so was she at the time) and clumsy, and they had had intercourse lying in the bed, while she had hoped for something similar to what she had observed, and which she had assumed to be anal intercourse.

A few sessions later she related in great detail one of her various prostitution fantasies. Up to this point, she had been generally rather reluctant to communicate their details, although she had referred to them.

She was a prostitute roaming the streets. She was picked up by a very tall young man who looked very virile. She explained to him that her fees were $10.00 for intercourse in his car, $20.00 if it was in her flat, and $50.00 for half an hour with her at her flat which would include whatever he wanted. He took the $10.00 job in his car. Once finished with him, she was roaming the streets again but this time she was hoping to be picked up by an old man. She finally found a plump man, well into middle age, who had dark skin and a plump face. (This description closely resembled that of her own father.) She took him to her flat. The man told her that she was wonderful and that he had enjoyed himself with her very much.

In the fantasy she was a very hygienic prostitute, always took a bath. The fantasy included many thoughts about what kind of clothes to wear in the "business" so that she could dress and undress quickly, wearing no underwear, etc. She thought that this particular fantasy was triggered by her mother telling her a few days before that, although she could not be sure yet, she might be pregnant. (Perhaps if she were an attractive, young prostitute father would impregnate her, too.) She actually was shocked at the thought that the mother could be pregnant; it was ridiculous. She was jealous that even her own mother might be having a baby while she was not even pregnant. Her surprise was compounded since she had lately convinced herself that father was by now impotent and no longer interested in sex. She concluded that obviously this was not the case.

She was well aware that the second man in the fantasy just described was her father, although she did not think of this at the time. Thinking more about it, she felt the fantasy was a way of paying back her mother, who she felt was behaving in too seductive a manner toward her boyfriend. Her mother had told him some dirty sexual jokes and the patient was upset by it. She thought her mother was loose, as father used to say, and that perhaps her mother was trying to seduce the patient's boyfriend. "She could, you know, she is very jolly and he likes that." She recalled, at this point, something an aunt had told her many years back, that is, that her father preferred the patient's sister to the patient because the sister resembled the mother very much, and her father, in spite of everything, was madly in love with his wife. She remembers this remark from her aunt as a tremendous blow to her.

Meanwhile, she had finally talked to her father and they were on "chatty terms now." Curiously, she did not find him as difficult as she used to, adding that she supposed that she knew more about her own fantasies about him and this was starting to work out.

By now, the relationship to the boyfriend was starting to be a little more devoid of the neurotic displacements (especially those of an oedipal nature) that made it so exciting and so tormenting. She still loved him, and very much wanted to marry him, but had come to the conclusion that, partly through her own fault, he was not willing to commit himself. He could have her any time he wanted, on whatever terms he wanted; why get married? the boyfriend would say quite openly to her. Further, because of her neurotic problems and masochistic tendencies, she had encouraged him to treat her badly, as a prostitute. Indeed, she had acted out many of these fantasies to such a point that they now had a very abnormal and unhealthy relationship. She did not know if the situation could change, but she did not want that any more. She wanted to marry and to have children. She had discussed this with him and, given his reluctance to make a commitment to her, she had decided, amidst much hesitation and ambivalence, to stop their relationship. This was a difficult time for the patient. Occasionally she would see him, at his insistence (which she welcomed) but would generally, though not always, stop short of intercourse and would not tolerate the type of abuse she had encouraged in the past. She was now convinced, I think quite rightly, that unless the relationship was placed on a different basis from before he would never marry her.

During this period her fantasy life greatly increased, as well as her masturbatory activities. Thus, for example, when she was again living at home, she had had a bad cold during the weekend. Her mother kept feeding her. It had been a pleasant weekend in spite of the discomfort caused by the cold. She read constantly and masturbated on different occasions while reading a book about prostitutes. The masturbatory fantasies (masturbation was always clitoridal) were as follows:

"I was a prostitute and there was this man who took the money from me, at least half of it. There were two other men hired by the pimp to beat those people who did not want to pay after using my services. The regular clients came first because that way I was not tired and gave them a better service. The new clients came afterwards. That day I asked the pimp: 'How many do I have today?' and he answered, 'twenty.' I thought that I would be very tired by the end but the pimp said just think of the money. The first client was a middle-aged fat man and the house where I saw myself during this fantasy was by the docks."

I reminded her that her father, like the pimp, had wanted to take her money away from her when she started working. Further, she had mentioned that when she was a child, the father would raid her savings bank frequently, in order to drink and gamble. It seemed then as if the pimp in the fantasy was associated with the father. She did not think of it at the time of the fantasy, but she thought I was right. In fact, she thought that the second client of the earlier fantasy had now become the pimp. Both could be easily identified as her father.

I said, too, that pimps are usually the "lovers" of the prostitute, to which she added: "Yes, I forgot, but toward the end of the fantasy, the pimp said to her that she looked very attractive. The pimp was very excited and finally took her to bed and had intercourse with her."

We could discuss now how very fond she had been of her father when she was a small girl. At some point, she had devised a fantasy to provide father with money and to keep him to herself. She rounded it out by adding that "actually money and the necessity of it is all father talks about."

Much of this material had by now come into the transference relationship in a variety of ways; I shall describe an instance or two. I should add that there was an interesting developmental sequence in this respect. Originally the patient had actively avoided including her analyst in any of her fantasy life; if anything came to mind, she would automatically reject it. At such times, one saw whatever fantasies she had about her analyst acted out outside the transference. She was very disturbed by any interpretation that attempted to show that what she was acting out outside the transference really belonged there.

In the second phase, she had conscious longings, wishes, fantasies, etc., regarding the therapist; these she could acknowledge to herself and to her analyst, but she essentially avoided referring to them. Unless the therapist spotted them she would tend not to communicate them (some of the reasons for this behavior are outside the scope of our interest here).

In a third phase, she had become more comfortable about making such communications more spontaneously. They were nevertheless accompanied by feelings of anxiety, guilt, shame, fears of being rejected, fears of seducing the therapist or being seduced by him, thus possibly disrupting her treatment, etc.

Thus, on a Monday session, she recalled the following dream:

"I came into the office for the daily analytic session and went to lie on the couch. After a while you were lying on the couch beside me telling me things, sweet sexual things, you know. Then we both were naked and having intercourse and the other things that go with it. Suddenly I realized it was 8:30 P.M. and was petrified because my boyfriend had been waiting for me outside the office. I went to the window to check if my boyfriend was still there and noticed that it was not really the street where this office is but one where I used to live when I was thirteen years old. When I turned back from the window, you were not you any longer but my boyfriend. All the time during the dream I had the feeling that you and I were married. Vaguely I remember too that some friends at some point in the dream were saying to me, 'You will end marrying your psychiatrist.' When I woke up from the dream I thought for a moment that I was in the office."

Though this is a complex and very overdetermined dream I shall only follow here those associative lines relevant to my subject matter.

The patient recalled having had intercourse with the boyfriend during the weekend at her parents' house. They were both naked, heard a noise and became frightened. The boyfriend dashed into the bathroom to get dressed and then came downstairs very pale. She was asked to associate with "having intercourse and the other things that go with it." She associated one of the primal scene observations she had already referred to some time ago, but the description was now more complete and meaningful. She said: "Father was talking to Mother all the time, by her neck. You see they thought I was sleeping. Father arrived home a bit drunk and started cuddling mother in my room where they were sleeping because there was a guest in their own room. He cuddled her and talked to her. How he had been excited and wanted to have intercourse with some young girls he had just seen at the seaside. They were at a fair by the big wheel and their skirts kept going up with the wind. 'Why did you not,' said Mother. Father replied, 'I kept it for home.' " She remembered mother's being excited but reluctant because the patient was "sleeping" in the room. She finally acquiesced and said "don't take long," to which father replied, "no I won't." Then he asked her if she was enjoying it but she did not reply. He said many sexy, loving things to her mother, something her boyfriend never did to her. She would have liked that, and "you did in the dream." She knew now that I stood for her father in the dream. She added, "that is why the street where this office was is the one I can see from my room at my parents' home. I think, too, that is why I wanted to have intercourse there with my boyfriend last weekend."

At other times she related overt sexual fantasies with the analyst. For example, she fantasized that when the analyst had been employed at the hospital where she was being seen, he had been told it would not be an easy job, since he would have to gratify all the wishes of his patients. "If they want to have intercourse with you, you have to do that, too," I was told. She thought this was a ridiculous and stupid fantasy. What would I think of her? Furthermore, as her longings for her father became clearer, she grew upset, thinking that only a mad person could possibly have such fantasies and wishes. She would then review the family history in terms of "madness," thinking that she might have inherited some of it. According to her, there were many disturbed people in her family, especially on the father's side. She claimed that her paternal great-grandfather had been in prison for having intercourse with his two daughters for many years. Her mother had told her this. She thought that perhaps it was for this reason that she had so much trouble with her sexual impulses, as well as having the many fantasies she had described about father. A paternal uncle of hers had committed suicide after having been accused by the police of molesting small girls. She was sure that there was something perverted that she had inherited. This thought frightened her, because she did not really want to be a prostitute or anything like that. She wanted very much to have just a nice family like anybody else. Yet, she gave examples of the way she demanded money from the boyfriend, as if he had to pay for her "services." They had gone to the movies and there was a long line. While waiting, she felt very hungry and demanded that the boyfriend give her some money so that she could eat while he waited in the line. She just had to have the money from him although she had money of her own. An unpleasant argument developed, but she finally got the money. From the cinema they went home and had intercourse (she knew this was to happen and that it was related to her asking for money). As soon as they finished she demanded that he give her five dollars "to pay for a theater ticket" she wanted to buy. At that point, she realized what she was doing. She stopped asking for money and developed a curious feeling of being on the one hand very frightened, and on the other very excited sexually—so much so that she seduced the boyfriend to have intercourse with her a second time.

She remembered another occasion, recently, when she was talking to another male friend about a party to which he had just invited her at his house. She had been behaving seductively and had overdone it. The boyfriend said, "Why are you always talking about sex or how exciting other males are for you when you talk to me?" She answered, very embarrassed, that it was her hobby. He said, "Well, try to behave like a decent woman at the party. It is only decent people who are going there, you know."

She continued that she had, in fact, felt compelled to ask her boyfriend for money again, although there was no reason whatsoever for her to do that. He asked what she wanted the money for. She said she wanted to repay her mother, whom she owed money, because things were tight at home. Father had been complaining how tight money was (10). The boyfriend knew this was not necessary and refused to give her anything. By now, he was very upset. He added that she ought to be more careful with her money and in any case she would be paid in a few days. She could give money to her mother then. She would not hear of it and started to complain and to cry. He said, "Stop the waterworks, it won't do you any good. I am not giving you any money." As was not uncommon, she became offensive to him. At that point, he jumped on her, pushed his trousers down, her skirt up, and forced her to have intercourse with him even though she was wearing an internal protection because she was having her period and did not want intercourse. She felt very humiliated since "she was being treated like a prostitute," but her first thought was "he owes me some money and must give it to me now." She then realized that she was behaving like the prostitute of her fantasy.

Her discussion of the above incident made clear that this type of interaction between them was, of late, not uncommon. She became aware that she had "trained" the boyfriend to behave like an animal, to abuse her sexually, to denigrate her, to treat her like a prostitute. He had not been like that at the beginning.

Obviously the boyfriend was capable of this behavior but the patient very skillfully provoked and elicited it. She was appalled as her realization of her contribution increased. Yet, though generally consciously offended by being treated in this way whenever it happened, she could realize that the whole thing was simul-

---

10. She did realize that she wanted to give the money to father through the mother, as was the case in her prostitution fantasies.

taneously exciting and that she was generally responsible for triggering it off.

Following the above sessions she referred to the situation at home. Her mother was doing her best to upset her father, mistreating him for no obvious reason. She had never noticed that before so clearly. Father said to the mother, in front of the patient and her boyfriend, that she was like that nowadays because she was jealous of the very good relationship he now had with his daughter (the patient). She had never been able to tolerate that.

The patient was flabbergasted and said that she had never noticed that herself, but she was now wondering. Her boyfriend said that her father was right. He had witnessed many such incidents and it was obvious to him that mother could not tolerate this.

When the time for her summer vacation was approaching, she became very concerned about the prospects of going by herself. She had planned to go with the boyfriend, but since the relationship was now stormy, she thought she might have to go on her own. She was concerned about her feelings of "not having control over my body" and prostituting herself during the holidays with any man she met. It will be remembered that this patient had been a bed-wetter until quite late in her life. She had rarely referred to this during much of her treatment. I suggested that the way she described her concerns about not having control over her body reminded me that she had been a bed-wetter and she must have felt then that she was not able to control her body in that way either. She agreed that it was very much the same fear and the same feeling of lack of control that she had had as a child. She referred to many incidents in her childhood when she wanted to "control herself" not to wet and had always failed. She found the whole thing quite frightening.

With her move back home, certain issues came to the foreground more clearly in the treatment, and it was more difficult for the patient to keep her distortions intact. One such area was that of the relationship to the mother, which she had managed to convince herself was a great deal better than it really was. She described, for example, an argument with the mother the previous evening. She had arrived home late and very hungry. The mother prepared something for her to eat but as she saw it, it was very little, badly done, and poorly presented.

She felt resentful and complained. The mother retorted that the patient had said she was not coming for dinner. She had already prepared the family meal and was now watching TV and was not willing to go to a lot of trouble again. In any case, she (the patient) was old enough to prepare something for herself. The patient stopped complaining but the mother continued arguing until, finally, the father, who had been listening patiently, got very angry with the patient. She could see she had been unreasonable. Yet if it had been her sister, mother would have prepared something decent for her, and would not say that she was old enough. She proceeded to abuse her mother in the session, feeling very jealous, envious, and resentful that mother would do things for the sister but not for her. The sister always got presents from mother, was taken out for meals, had her bed made by the mother. She hated her mother and wished for her death.

As time went by the importance of the oral fixation in this patient became more and more clear. It seemed possible to me that the mother had suffered a postpartum depression after the patient's birth, as after that of the sister. The patient may have been somewhat neglected as a baby and left to suffer from hunger as the result of it. (This indeed seemed to have been the case. The patient made some inquiries about this, although the mother had been very reluctant to discuss it.) She knew that at a later stage she had eaten excessively and was a very fat child, in contrast to her sister, who had always been very slim and looked very pretty. As time went by, it became clear that the sister, too, had problems in this area and had, on more than one occasion, suffered from what impressed me as a very mild form of anorexia nervosa.

For the patient food had always been extraordinarily important and we have seen examples of it in her present symptoms and daily life. One of her many difficulties with her boyfriends was that she frequently gave them the role of a good mother who feeds her baby generously, who always gratifies her every wish (as she thought her mother did with her sister) gives her presents constantly, and especially "prefers" no rivals to her. She tried to recreate with her boyfriends an idealized relationship to a good pre-oedipal mother. Naturally, no boyfriend was capable of playing this role for her, nor could they understand much of her behavior when she reacted to frustration with disappointment, rage, and demands that were somewhat childish, frequently irrational, and generally excessive. Thus, her oedipal fantasies and longings that were acted out in her relationships to males were further compounded and complicated by the extraneous influences of the oral and anal fixations and the pre-oedipal elements of the relationship to the mother. Since these influences contaminated the phallic-oedipal and oedipal constellations of this patient, they tended to obscure the forms that the clinical expression of the latter took. At times, the intensity of the oral and/or anal needs was so great that they more or less overlay the oedipal manifestations, which, at that point, became essentially the vehicles for acting out those needs, rather than something with primary significance itself. Oedipal language became the form of expression of concerns and needs from the oral and anal phases that were essentially pre-oedipal (Nagera, 1966).

As the analysis progressed, the patient recovered many conscious death wishes about her mother from her childhood, more especially from the ages of ten to twelve or thirteen years. In those days, there was much talk of divorce at home because her father was accusing the mother of being friendly with a man. She remembered, at the time, there was another man about whom father apparently did not know. This one used to come to the house when the father was not there. Father was now working in another town and only came home for weekends. This man was very "friendly" to the mother. The patient suspected that he probably was mother's lover. This was the time when she had fantasies that mother would leave and she would look after her father, and, furthermore, she had active death wishes against the mother. Slowly, other components of this situation emerged. She was frightened, too, that mother would leave with this man and abandon her. This fear, although essentially based on pre-oedipal elements, contained, as well, phallic-oedipal (first stage) elements. Thus, she remembered being resentful that mother needed this friend while father was away and was not just content with the patient's company and presence. She remembered envying these men in whom the mother was so interested—she felt, at her expense. On occasion she thought that if she had been a boy, mother would not need this man. She wished she were a boy and once in a while resented her father's coming home weekends because he, too, took all the mother's attention away from her. She hated him for this and yet simultaneously she longed for him, felt sorry for him, and wanted to take the mother's place in the relationship to the father.

It seems that this patient's main fixation was at the oedipal phase, second stage (positions [b] and [d] in Figure 2), with the father as the main object of her positive libidinal cathexis and the mother as the rival. Many of her relationships, behavior, symptoms, fantasies, needs, conflicts, etc., are clearly the expression of that fixation. The special form taken by her fantasies (i.e., of prostitution) can be understood in terms of her life experience, the vicissitudes of the parental relationship and interactions, and their effect on the growing girl. They gave the patient "models" for identification. She elaborated on all of these the fabric of her neuroses, her character structure, her very life style, ideals, and goals. The prostitution fantasy shows the identification with the "prostitute" mother, which is, in fact, a passive-feminine identification of sorts. That father could be made into her gigolo, and by such means, she could provide him with as much money as he wanted, further reinforced this type of fantasy and the many variations of acting-out behavior that went with it.

Yet, as we have seen, she had relevant though relatively less important fixations at the phallic-oedipal phase, first stage (positions [a] and [c] in figure 2), with the mother as the object of her positive libidinal cathexis and the father and males in general as rivals. We have seen the evidence for this in her present life and her interest, for example, in her girlfriend, A., the model, in her jealousy of A.'s attraction to males, including her own boyfriend. Yet, the material clearly and consistently shows that disappointment with a male object, or facts or events that increased her insecurity as a desirable feminine object tended temporarily to increase and reinforce her active-masculine wishes.

At such points she wanted to be a boy and had a boy's longings for girls, a phenomenon that otherwise did not appear to be primary. Clearly, too, this was much more ego dystonic than her "promiscuous" behavior or prostitution fantasies. This fixation (and whatever penis envy was observable) was the result of both parents' disappointment with her sex and more particularly of the mother's clear preference for little boys.

This problem was further compounded by the difficulties, rejections, and disappointments she experienced during her oedipal stage. We must take into account that the patient at six years of age had to take the mother's role to a considerable degree because of her own mother's prolonged postpartum depression. Moves toward the father, which he encouraged when the relationship to his wife deteriorated, usually ended in a massive rejection when the situation improved with his wife. This constant uncertainty greatly stimulated the little girl and contributed to her fixation at the oedipal phase (second stage), while simultaneously reinforcing the defensive regressive tendencies to the less important fixation at the first stage.

Beyond that, we have seen, too, how oral and anal components not only influenced the shape taken by the phallic-oedipal and oedipal stages and its different forms of expression, but also how, at times, these needs and conflicts were expressed in phallic-oedipal and oedipal language, thus complicating a clear clinical understanding of the patient. Her basic sexual position can be seen essentially as passive-feminine. Here again the defensive move to an active-masculine one seemed always due to a disappointment with male objects. This is very reminiscent of her childhood situation when she was forced to turn back again to mother after father's massive rejection of her. These rejections always followed a period when the father was seductive of the little girl.

Child Cases

Direct observations of children offer convincing evidence of the different stages described. They demonstrate too the rather typical manifestations of these phases in behavior, fantasy, play and speech.

A few examples of the behavior of children during the phallic-oedipal and oedipal phases follow. But first we need to distinguish clinically that behavior from the superficially similar one that is to be observed in toddlers.

Child Case 1

S. is a brown-eyed, brown-haired, two-and-a-half-year-old girl. She is adopted and has an older sibling, P., who is eight and a half.

She is a member of our toddler group for normal children and though she is intelligent, her development, especially in the psychosexual sense, seems to be lagging behind somewhat. Thus, for example, she shows no interest in the typical play with dolls that usually begins around this age or shortly thereafter. Playing house, mother, wife, caring for dolls, etc., is absent from her behavior. She will pick up dolls, but only to examine them generally and their bodies in particular, move their arms and legs around, etc., as younger toddlers tend to do. This play is done always in isolation from peers, in contrast to truly oedipal children who, if given the opportunity, do enjoy interacting with one another, taking roles in cooperative play such as that of the mother, sister, father, baby, etc., and generally play-acting family life. Typically, the activities of phallic-oedipal children with dolls are accompanied by talking, by descriptive accounts of what is happening, etc. By themselves they will play several roles simultaneously, that is, they will mimic first the mother and then the child, or the baby's response to the mother, etc. S. is as yet incapable of this type of behavior.

She still displays negativistic, obstinate anal behavior with temper tantrums, which shows clearly that her phase dominance is essentially at the anal stage.

Yet, the mother stated that S. had begun playing "under covers in bed" with her brother. She concluded, I think rightly, that it was essentially some kind of hide and seek game. "S. is at the moment high on that kind of activity," the mother stated. It was noticed that S.'s mother was inappropriately giggling while describing this play of her children under the covers in bed.

Through further questioning we found that the mother quite actively encourages the children to sleep together. She especially encourages S. to go into her brother's bed. The brother will tolerate this for a few minutes, but will soon be yelling for his sister to be removed from his bed. The mother then explained that she too used to sleep in her brother's bed when she was a child.

The mother asserted, in responding to the interviewer's questions, that S. was well aware of sexual differences. S. and her brother are bathed together and she "grabs him and teases him, laughing while she is doing this." (The mother is very anxious at this point.) The mother handles this situation by asking the boy if he wants to cover himself with a washrag. She is concerned that perhaps this type of experience may not be too good for S., but on the other hand, *she does not wish to ruin their fun.* Further exploration of this brought to light that she too used to bathe with her brother.

For the inexperienced, some of the behavior described might be taken as oedipal. Yet, as we have seen above, S. is not anywhere near that stage, in spite of being at an age where some manifestations of the move into a phallic-oedipal situation start to become visible.

Essentially, it seems reasonable to conclude that the mother is re-enacting her own unconscious conflicts and wishes through the agency of her children and the behavior that she encourages in them. In this sense it is of interest that the mother is preoccupied with the effects of these "games" on S., but gives no thought to its effects on her son.

S. has clearly been stimulated prematurely in this regard and though her behavior at this point cannot be regarded as penis envy, it might well constitute the basis of it at a later date as she continues to develop. We are as well aware of the retrospective traumatic effects of events of this type in some children as they reach those phases of development where the behavior may acquire special and very significant meanings. Be that as it may, this case illustrates as well how the psychopathology or the unresolved unconscious conflicts of the mother may influence the child's development. It may prematurely encourage behaviors that may well prove detrimental when the time to negotiate the phallic-oedipal (first stage) and the oedipal phase (second stage) arrives.

Child Case 2

P. is a very bright girl, four years and two months old, attending nursery school for normal children. She is verbal, outgoing and relates well with peers and staff. She is very sensitive and has already a well-developed empathic capacity. She shows concern for her peers if they get hurt or look sad.

P.'s baby brother M. was born when she was two years and ten months of age. Though by now she occasionally talks about him in a positive way, she had very marked difficulties accepting him at the beginning. In the nursery and at home she talked a great deal about how much she hated him, about her wish that the parents would give him away, or abandon him, leaving him alone for ever. During this time, she was seen playing (at the nursery) in the doll corner where she would feed the dolls, bathe them and take them for rides on the rocking boat. She frequently talks to the dolls and was overheard saying to them, "You know babies can get killed."

Around this time too, she developed an imaginary companion by the name of "Purple Dragon" who would kill babies, mommies and daddies. She was easily frustrated and had a lot of trouble sharing and taking turns, not an uncommon reaction for young nursery school children after the birth of a sibling. When new children joined the nursery (twin boys) she was very hostile to them, telling the boys, "I don't like you, stay away from me." She was thus displacing her sibling rivalry and hostility to new additions to the nursery school just as she resented the arrival of her baby brother.

At home too, the mother reported prolonged conversations between P. and "Purple Dragon" while P. was in her bedroom. Mostly they concerned her very angry feelings about her baby brother and in particular her mother, to whom she could be very hostile. As you would expect "Purple Dragon" slept under her bed and occupied a space at the dining table since P. insisted that he must have his meals with the family.

Generally speaking she can use play very constructively to deal with her anxieties. She accompanies her play-acting with meaningful verbalizations. She used to assume the role of the mother, but now makes it clear that she is the wife asking one of the boys to be the husband. Frequently, she becomes bossy and demanding during this play. At times she is so overbearing in her hugging, kissing and chasing of the boys that they get annoyed at her, asking her to stop. This in turn, annoys her.

During the house play she freely verbalizes that she is pregnant, will have lots of babies, etc. On occasions she makes herself ready to go to the hospital to have her babies, while placing two dolls under her dress. A little later she told the teacher she had twins, but *they were twin girls.*

She expressed concerns that her cat could not have kittens since it had a special operation. The next day she told the teacher that Sugar and Spice (cats) had gotten together and Sugar was now pregnant. She once stated to the teacher, "You know, Mrs. D., when I get to be 13 years old, I am going to get pregnant. The baby is going to grow in my stomach."

Like most children going through this phase, P. has nightmares consisting of monsters chasing and eating her up.

I think most readers of this material probably will agree that P. essentially is in the oedipal phase (second stage). Unfortunately, she has significant conflicts that interfere with a clear dominance of that stage. They tend to induce relatively easy regressive moves from a passive-feminine identification (typical for the oedipal-phase) into an active-masculine one, with clear signs of penis envy as a source of interference.

Thus, it is not uncommon while she is playing with the dolls (acting out the part of the mother, caring for her babies) that something will happen that triggers her dissatisfaction with that role.

Example 1: P. was mothering a doll, hugging it. She saw two of the boys playing cowboys. She quickly announced that she was a cowlady, adding in a louder voice that she was a cow-woman until finally, in a very loud voice she claimed that she was a cowboy too.

I think the example shows how her more passive-feminine interests and identifications are easily interfered with by a still very active wish to be a boy, shown by her competing with them, identifying with them and wanting to be accepted by them as another boy, in this case a "cowboy."

Example 2: P. and another girl were dressed up as ladies (grown-up shoes and hats, etc.). They started to object to three boys that were playing house and using cooking utensils. The girls stated that this was girls' stuff, not really for boys. At this point the boys pretended to become firemen who squirted the girls with their hoses in order to protect their house and their cooking utensils. P. soon took off her feminine "attire," that is took off her grown-up dress, hat, etc., and proceeded to announce loudly, "I am Superman . . . I am Superman . . . I know it!"

We have described earlier the adult equivalents and manifestations of this type of early conflict and fixation point. Women, though strongly desiring a relationship with males, a family, children, etc., find themselves quickly triggered into a very active competitive and castrating situation toward their male friends. Usually, the relationship sours and ends in a profound disappointment for both parties. This type of woman is not infrequently aware of the conflict between her longings for a feminine role and her dissatisfaction with it. They find themselves forever seeking a substitute for the "valuable" and "absent" penis and/or a masculine position.

P. may well be an example of only girls for whom the birth of a sibling, especially a boy, between the ages of two and a half and four or thereabouts, combines a sudden spurt of sibling rivalry, penis envy and a loss of some of the mother's attention (all of which tend to potentiate each other) evokes difficulties in moving cleanly out of the phallic-oedipal phase (first stage) and into the oedipal phase (second stage).

As we have seen, P. is very resentful of both the baby brother and the mother, presumably on several grounds. Firstly, P. was not enough and thus mother "brought" another baby with the resultant and unavoidable disruption in P.'s unique relationship with her. Further, it was a baby boy. Given the way young children think, P. may well have concluded that "boys" are "better" than girls, thus explaining why mother was not satisfied with just her. Finally, but related to the above, P. may well be very annoyed with the mother because she did not "make" her a boy, but a girl.

With P. the above considerations can only be speculative since we have to rely on direct observations and not on treatment material. Yet the analytic treatment of young girls and adult females frequently demonstrates the importance of the fantasies described above. It seems a reasonable assumption to consider the birth of her baby brother, among other things, as one of the possible explanations for the difficulties P. is confronting in assuming a dominant, firm position in the oedipal phase (second stage).

I have stressed that other factors are concerned because the phenomenon described is not universal. As we will see in the example that follows, the birth of a sibling will not always have such a disruptive effect. The quality and intensity of the previous relationship to the mother, intensity of the "loss of mothering" as experienced by the child, the quality of the relationship to the father, the degree of ego development, the nature of the child's fantasies, etc., play significant and at times decisive roles in the fate of such events.

Child Case 3

B. is a cute, four-and-a-half-year-old, petite girl with long brown hair. She joined the nursery school a year ago. She has a younger brother born when she was two and a half. She did not show any anxiety about separating from the mother at the time of entry into the Child Psychoanalytic Study Program nursery school. Nevertheless, she was concerned about her younger brother D., going occasionally into the observation room with a toy for him, as if making sure that he too had something special to play with while she enjoyed herself in the nursery. I should explain that at the time of entry into our nursery school setting, mothers (in this case mother and younger brother) are allowed to stay in the observation room (next to the nursery) until we can ascertain that the child can separate without anxiety.

The mother described how B. for some time before entering the nursery was always playing house at home and how "she always wanted to be the daddy." Both mother and father agreed that in those days B. often "imitated her dad." For example, she used to "smoke a pipe" around the house like her father. At around this time too (B. was about three) she was clearly interested in sexual differences. She told her father, "You have a big one (penis) and D. has a little one." Earlier on she had told the father, "I come up to your penis."

When B. was over two years of age the mother was observing (through her living-room window) how B. played with several other children in their communal courtyard. The boys were urinating on a tree in the courtyard, which made the girls obviously angry because they could not do it. "They were angry and tugging at the skin between their legs!"

As can be seen in the above material, B. was at this time clearly in the phallic-oedipal position (first stage). This started to change shortly before she joined the nursery school. At that time she told her father, "I'd like to marry you, Daddy, but I think I will marry T. O. (a neighborhood boy)." By the time she joined the nursery and quickly thereafter, B. had unequivocally moved into the oedipal position (second stage), as the material following demonstrates.

Much of B.'s play in the nursery is centered upon the doll corner, where she spends much time cooking, taking care of the dolls, talking on the phone to her friends, etc. It is very apparent that B.'s mannerisms and speech are remarkably like those of her mother.

It has been noticed that the quality of her doll play has changed significantly. As she herself says, the dolls are now "real babies" and get treated as such, with much care and tenderness. B. talks a great deal about getting married, being pregnant and about going to the hospital to deliver her babies. B. is described as somewhat seductive toward male peers with much hugging, kissing and touching of the boys. Yet the boys do not seem resentful of it, in contrast with the earlier example, P., where the boys are distinctly uncomfortable and reject P.

B. has told T. (a nursery school peer) that they are going to get married when they grow up. At times she tells the teacher that she had just come from the hospital from having her baby;

at others she said, "I have to feed my baby," proceeding to pull up her top while pretending to nurse her baby. She is not uncomfortable when the boys watch her while she pretends to nurse.

She is seen to masturbate frequently, especially so when she sits near male peers. She has nightmares not infrequently, as would be expected for a child of her age and stage of development. Typically, in her nightmares, she is pursued by threatening monsters.

This child and the one in the earlier example are playmates at the nursery school and frequently share their play with dolls. Though to the unskilled observer their behavior looks very similar, there are very significant differences between the two of them. B.'s mothering of the dolls is full of positive maternal qualities. She is gentle and tender when manipulating her babies. Though she too has a younger baby brother like P., she seems to have appropriately mastered her sibling rivalry after an appropriate period of time and no obvious signs of penis envy or of the wish to be a boy are observed, in sharp contrast with P. There is no hostility, no ambivalence toward her "babies" while the other child, P., handles them abruptly, in an unfeminine, careless, untender manner, and is curt with them, occasionally threatening that "babies can get killed."

B. is not distracted from her positive passive feminine identification and play by threats from the boys or by "boyish" activities. This again is in sharp contrast to P., whose envy and wish to be like the boys is easily aroused, to the point that she abandons her mothering roles in attempting to become one of the boys. B. lets the boys be boys while she continues quite satisfied to play-act with great pleasure her passive-feminine fantasies and well established identifications.

In short, with B. the oedipal phase (second stage) is phase-dominant, with no significant regressions. B.'s passive-feminine identifications seem well established and are essentially non-conflictual.

This brief history shows her quick progression through the phallic-oedipal phase (first stage) and into the oedipal phase (second stage). As we have seen, she seems already capable of

displacing her interest in her father to other males without difficulty. This capacity will serve her well when the time for the
resolution of her oedipus complex arrives.

Child Case 4

Clinically, we come across many adult cases of various types
which seem best explained by a fixation at the oedipal phase,
second stage. In our Adult Case #2 we saw the clinical manifestations of this. These are women who have never abandoned the
infantile longing to "marry" their fathers. Naturally, no men
around them are capable of fulfilling this infantile wish. Some
among them never marry. Others do marry and have very un-
successful marriages, since they do not really want a husband,
but a father. Naturally, most men expect to acquire a wife and
not a daughter, a situation that leads to much unhappiness and
disharmony. Still others do clearly marry men that are trans-
parent images of their fathers. They may be, for example, much
older, have the same professional background as their fathers, etc.

It is self-evident that some elements of the oedipal phase and
struggles are more or less significant determinants of people's
object choices. The distancing from the actual infantile libidinal
longings and the degree of neutralization achieved will significantly influence the success or failure of such choices. In the first
case the choice will be highly conflictual and sooner or later will
show itself. In the second case the same model (father or mother)
can be used, but the libidinal longings have been sufficiently
neutralized. Though the object choice has been strongly influenced by the father as a "desirable" model, the situation is not
likely to become highly conflictual if the appropriate degree of
neutralization of the infantile wishes has been achieved.

Clearly, all that was described above applies similarly in the
case of males.

This example, one of many, illustrates in the actual behavior
of the young child the point at which the fixation takes place,
whatever the reasons leading to it. One of the necessary steps in
the final resolution of the oedipal phase (second stage) is the
ability to displace the infantile longings for the father, in the
case of the normal girl, and for the mother in the case of the

normal boy, to a nonincestuous, suitable object of the appropriate sex. Such a sequence is easily observed in embryo, for example, in a nursery school setting, and we have already given examples of this.

T. is five years and two months old. She spends a great deal of time in the doll corner of the nursery school. She cooks, cleans, takes care of the dolls, and frequently pretends to phone her father and on occasion her Uncle F. In house play she will consistently refuse to assume roles such as that of the baby, sister, etc., if peers try to assign them to her. She will only accept that of the wife. Peers will frequently suggest as the game develops that since T. is the wife, any one of the boys in the group should be her husband. She consistently and obstinately refuses accepting any of her peers as the husband, always adding in strong terms, "My Dad is my husband."

It is clear that at this point in her development any other object choice, even in play-acting, is totally unacceptable to her. If the bulk of her infantile wishes, longings and fantasies were to remain where they are now as she moves along developmentally, she would become one of the adult females with difficulties in object choice described above. T. is quite likely, as her development proceeds, to accept a substitute for the father, first in the form of a peer in her play-acting role of the wife, and later on in life in the form of a real non-incestuous object.

Many children between three and four already show this capacity, accepting a peer in their play-acting as the husband as if they have come to terms in some form with the fact that they cannot marry their fathers. Others like B., Case 3 above, show clearly the transition from the one stage to the other. You will remember that B. said to her father, "I'd like to marry you, Daddy, but I think I'll marry T. (a neighborhood peer)."

CHAPTER 12

The Timing of the Phallic-Oedipal and Oedipal Phases

The timing of the negative or inverted complex (in my terminology: phallic-oedipal, first stage) in the girl, and that of her move to the positive attachment to the father (second stage) require some elucidation. Bonaparte (1953, p. 42) stated that

the positive oedipus complex in the girl, passively oriented towards the father, must chronologically establish itself at least as early as does the boy's positive oedipus complex towards the mother, and still more so if earlier observations of coitus, for instance, have made the child realize the differences between the sexes.

My own observations at the Hampstead Clinic and in the Child Psychoanalytic Study Program at the University of Michigan contradict Bonaparte's timetable. According to my experience boys and girls reach the stage of the phallic-oedipal (first stage) attachment to the mother with the father as the rival (in earlier terminology, the negative or inverted complex for the girl, the positive complex for the boy) at about the same time, usually around the beginning of the third year of life. The boy usually expends something like two years in this phase and normally by the fifth year of life is fairly advanced on the road to latency, though full dominance of the phase may only come some time later.

My observations in girls seem to demonstrate that after entering into the phallic-oedipal attachment to the mother the girl remains in that phase for a period that oscillates between one and two years, mostly about one year. Frequently by the beginning of the fourth year the girl shows clear manifestations of a fluid transitional stage: both the negative and positive complexes are simultaneously present and unstable in their relationship. From here onwards, all going well, she moves more and more into the positive complex (oedipal phase, second stage), though manifestations of the negative complex do not always disappear completely from the picture. This can be explained partly as the result of the intense telescoping of the two phases—the differentiation between them must be achieved in a limited period of time—and partly by the intrinsic difficulties in the detachment of cathexis from the original objects.

Very frequently the girl expends the fourth year of her life at the peak of her positive oedipal attachment to the father but usually by the fifth year she starts increasingly to show the advances to the latency period. I believe that this end of the scale is not so simple, clearcut and definite as it is frequently supposed. By the sixth year in any case the girl is usually well established in latency.

In general my observations lead me to conclude that the girl has to go through the two stages of her oedipal development (negative and positive) in approximately the same time that the boy spends in his positive oedipal attachment to the mother.

I shall add that with the move towards the father—but only if the move is toward the positive oedipal attachment to him and not, for example, the one that may occur in the case of the inverted complex, first stage (see Figure 2)—there is usually a marked reduction or suppression of clitoridal activity. Up to a point this corresponds with the neutralization or sublimation in the boy of the phallic impulses directed toward the mother as the phase comes to an end. But even when this has happened the boy retains a clear preference and closeness to his mother which is in itself not incompatible with a normal period of latency. At puberty there is frequently a highly conflictive reactivation of the phallic impulses towards the mother. These are frequently expressed in a displaced manner in masturbatory fantasies that may involve more distant relatives than the mother or other mother substitutes. The girl, on the other hand, represses as well her phallic (clitoridal) impulses when she takes the father as an object in normal development, but the unconscious content of the fantasies show, as in some of the examples above, that the relationship remains highly sexualized for a short time. Yet though the vagina may play some role in fantasies it makes no actual physical contribution for a long time (see Chapter 10). Then there is a desexualization of the relationship to the father allowing the normal girl a continued preference for him that is in no way incompatible with a normal latency. In both the boy and the girl, what interferes with the latency period is the insufficient desexualization of the relationship to the parent chosen.

It is not always easy to distinguish between the manifestations of the earlier oral and anal attachment to the mother and those that correspond to the phallic-oedipal attachment to her, but I believe such a distinction is possible. For this purpose one has to concentrate one's attention at the point at which behavioral manifestations, symptoms, fantasies, play, etc., start to appear in terms of *triangular relationships*. This is the point at which the father has become not just an interference in the relationship to the mother, but a true rival in the phallic-oedipal sense. It is true nevertheless that the manifestations of rivalry with the father are generally not so marked in girls as they are in boys. This fact contributes to the difficulties of the assessment, but we are helped by observing closely instead the very obvious manifestations of the "castration complex" in girls, including their penis envy. At times, a new wave of masturbation (various types of it) may be apparent and accompany all the above manifestations. All these must alert us to the fact that the phallic zone is acquiring dominance and that the phallic-oedipal relationships to the mother is already operative or must soon be so. There are as well and for a short time slightly distorted manifestations of phallic exhibitionism at this stage (in an attempt to compensate for their awareness of the small size of the clitoris) with frequent cries, generally to the mother, such as "Mummy, look at my long nose," or "Haven't I got long ears, Mummy?" or "Look at my long stick" (when one has been found), etc., the meaning of which will be discussed.

It is necessary to realize as well, that quite apart from the above mentioned factors there are a number of other elements that influence the form of expression of the phallic-oedipal attachment to the mother in the case of the girl. For example, the balance between activity and passivity is not exactly the same in boys and girls. In the latter and in spite of the dominance of the active-masculine components during the phase under discussion the overall balance, in relative terms, is not as markedly active when compared with most boys. There are, of course, occasional exceptions to the rule, in which case the assessment does not present any difficulties. Not infrequently it is these same girls that behave in a strikingly tomboyish manner during the latency period. This behavior can be transitory or permanent in character, but in either case points to the intensity of the fixation to an active-masculine sexual position and to the penis envy conflict.

Further, Freud (1931, p. 225) has shown that the rivalry with the father for the affection of the mother during the girl's phallic-oedipal attachment to her never reaches the intensity that it does in the boy.

Perhaps even more important is the fact that with the phase dominance of the phallic (clitoridal) stage and the increased cathexis of the organ there is almost simultaneously the realization of its organic "inferiority." This is such a narcissistic blow to the girl that it contributes in good measure to the abandonment of the attachment to the mother, up to this point intense, and leads the fight against masturbation. I further believe that the girl's realization of her "physical inferiority" forces on her a certain modesty and restraint in the phallic claims for the mother; hence its frequently distorted manifestations in bids for the mother's admiration on the basis of her long nose, long tongue, long ears, long hands, long hair, long fingers, long feet, long sticks, etc. It forces her too to divert much of her energies in various directions in an attempt to explain the "physical inferiority."

Much of the obscurity introduced by all these factors in the assessment of the phallic-oedipal girl's attachment to the mother becomes patently clear in the case of female adults. There the conflict may have finally settled around its specific nuclei and many of the distracting elements characteristic of the early developmental stages with its multiple simultaneous processes have been left behind. Through the analysis of adult females with certain forms of sexual disturbances we can reconstruct in retrospect many of these earlier developmental disturbances. We can ascertain the extent of the phallic-oedipal attachment to the mother from an active-masculine position with all its consequences for later development and the sexual position finally reached. For example, some female homosexuals who must play a masculine role in their homosexual relationships attach to themselves phallic-like objects in order to penetrate their passive partners or use their fingers, hands, etc., as a penis substitute.

Jones (1923) and Flügel (1925) long ago pointed out the use of the tongue as a substitute for the penis. The identification tongue = penis, according to Jones (1927), in some female homosexuals reaches "a quite extraordinary degree of completeness." In such cases the tongue takes over the role of the penis in the homosexual relationship. The little girl's cry, "Mummy, look at my big tongue," can in this light be understood in its true significance, that is, "Mummy, will this be a satisfactory substitute for my missing penis?" Some such homosexuals fixated at this stage fulfill these early fantasies by finding in later life a *mother-substitute* that is satisfied with a *penis substitute*.

Clinical Illustrations

Two of the three examples that follow illustrate the clinical manifestations observed during the *transitional period* that exists between the move from the phallic-oedipal attachment to the mother (first stage) to the oedipal attachment to the father (second stage), including the concomitant changes in the girl's sexual position. The last of the three cases shows a slightly older girl still firmly established in the second stage of her oedipal development.

Example 1

P. is a small, attractive, self-willed little girl of three years and ten months. She is a member of our nursery school and has two siblings, both boys. One is eighteen months younger and the other is a baby five months old.

Between P. and her father there is a close flirtatious relationship that may well have helped to stimulate the beginnings of the positive attachment to him somewhat earlier than usual. Another contributory factor here may have been her disappointment with the mother because of the birth of the second baby brother a few months before. Since then she has given signs of an increased fantasy life involving the father while it is still similarly clear that she is at best in a transitional stage, with much of her drive organization attached to the mother in a phallic-oedipal and pre-oedipal fashion. Similarly, she has not completely abandoned the wish for a penis, though she gives few signs of penis envy at this time.

At three years and four months, coinciding with the birth of her last sibling, she told one of the teachers at the nursery a long story of how her Daddy had taken her to a shop (The Sound of Music). She had gone alone with her Daddy, not with her Mummy, and Daddy had even bought her an ice cream. The story became much more meaningful when one knows that this was a product of her fantasy and not a real event. By the age of three years and ten months during an intelligence test she referred to going away with Daddy to Canada (probably a fantasy). After the test, she was given a box with toys to play and she picked out the family dolls, the bed and the bath. She said the little girl was in the bath and the father was looking after her tenderly. Then the father admonished the little girl not to jump on the mother's bed or make it untidy but the little girl made the parents' bed untidy by jumping on it, disappearing afterwards in the woods. Then P. put father to bed in the bed, mother to bed in the bath and the little girl next to the father's bed on the floor, clearly showing in this play the content of her oedipal fantasies and the wish to separate father and mother, and to take the latter's place. The conflict here is seen in the little girl not being actually in bed with the father as the mother would, but next to the bed on the floor.

There are indications as well that she identifies with the mother, possibly in a passive-feminine role: she insists that she looks like her mother, while the siblings look like father. Similarly, during the test (opposite analogies test) she answered: "a brother is a boy, a sister is a . . ." and "a father is a man, a mother is . . . a girl." At this point she started a little song about boys not being girls, girls not being boys. The test-maker wondered what was "better." She replied, "Girls are better, they do not fight," but after a second's pause she added, "My mummy is going to give me a water pistol for my birthday."

The sequence of events shows the fluidity between what looks like the beginning of passive-feminine identifications and the still present wish for a penis (1).

Example 2

The following case is of a little girl, G., who at the age of four and a half already shows evident signs of advancing quickly from the phallic-oedipal position (first stage), to the oedipal position (second stage). Naturally, since much of her drive organization is still at a transitional point between the two we can observe the attachment to the mother and some interest in "tails," their sizes and the possible damaging effects of being in contact with one.

The mother described G. as very fond of her father *at the moment,* often flinging her arms around him and stating that she loves him. Further she has developed recently the habit of coming into the parents' bed every morning to cuddle with the father, but when he gets up she still turns around and cuddles with mother. The child has always demanded love from both parents, but the last few months she makes it clear that she loves mummy very much, but she really loves daddy just a little more. Both father and mother overstimulate the child and encourage this behavior (perhaps more especially the mother) and a great

---

1. I am grateful to the Educational Unit and more especially to Miss Edgecumbe, Mrs. Friedman and Miss Putzel for the facilities to study and use their material.

deal of kissing and cuddling goes on in bed. There can be no question that the present kissing and cuddling are essentially related to the phallic-oedipal and oedipal phases, though in such a young child there are always pre-phallic elements involved. This is demonstrated by the nature of some of her ego fantasies that she has verbalized occasionally, such as her comment that she would "want to give her wee-wee to daddy but it is too small for him." Similarly, she complained recently that her wee-wee was sore and when the mother offered her cream she wanted the father to be present and hold her legs. More recently G. has "fallen in love" with a boy at school whom she thinks is marvelous.

An important question of differential diagnosis in this case concerns the need to ascertain if in such a young girl the manifestations of her positive attachment to the father correspond to the positive complex of the second stage (oedipal) or to the negative complex of the first stage (phallic-oedipal) since in both cases the father is cathected positively by the feminine elements of the girl's bisexual constitution. The fact that in quantitative terms the preference is clearly for the father and not the mother may point to the positive complex, second stage. That these manifestations are not the expression of the inverted complex, first stage, can be ascertained by the content of her fantasies, where she seems to accept a passive-feminine position that could not correspond with the inverted complex of the first stage.

Further support for all the above can be seen in a fantasy she produced as a reaction to a card (rabbit sitting up in bed in a shadowy room with the door open) during her psychological test. She said, "The bunny was in the bed and mummy and daddy were downstairs and there's father bunny's bed, and I don't know where mother bunny's bed is, and I think I can see somebody like father walking in. And father bunny gets into his bed and baby bunny is awake and should be asleep shouldn't *she, he,* and father bunny might jump into baby bear's bed instead of his own. Next, father bear might jump into his own bed instead of baby bear's. I can see a bit broke. Door open a bit. Don't know what happens next . . . I think father bear is going to have a party with mother bear."

The oedipal wishes (positive complex, second stage) are quite plain in the story. Sexuality is still conceived as something aggressive and somewhat violent but the wish to have the father come to her while mother is away seems evident. Somebody interrupts the fantasy (obviously mother) and she let them carry on with their "party." Further, concern about the penis and what it can do to the female is shown in her reaction to another card. She remarked, "Look at his long tail, funny old tail! . . . The tail somebody could hold onto. *The tail could go in somebody's eye and hurt them.*" This comment linked with the above wish of being attacked by the father suggests, I believe, that her concern with the tail is not out of penis envy but of what father's tail can do to her small wee-wee (see above). This case and others observed showed that in a number of girls the move into the second stage of their oedipal development is already apparent as early as the beginning of the fourth year of life, as mentioned earlier. I should expect the positive attachment to the father to be present sometime during the fourth year of life if development has proceeded normally. I am talking of phase dominance here, since some manifestations of interest in the father are normally to be seen even during the phallic-oedipal attachment to the mother (first stage).

Example 3

W. was five years and nine months of age at the time of the diagnostic interview. She was described as quite good-looking with long, dark hair, dark eyes and regular features.

The mother said that W. is "very keen on her father" but not very responsive to her. She further remarked that when W. is bathed together with her brother, S. (three years younger), she becomes "very sensual" and will try to handle his genitals. This behavior, to my mind, shows how advanced she is in her passive-feminine development. She does not react as younger girls may with curiosity, questioning, aggression, disappointment or envy. She is sexually excited by their sight and wishes to handle them.

The father described her as "very feminine," liking to use the mother's lipstick, examining herself in the mirror, thrilled with new clothes, etc. The father too described her as very affectionate toward him, always welcoming him very especially when he arrives home in the evening. She frequently writes letters to him and wraps up presents for him. Further, she likes to get into bed with father in the mornings, cuddling up to him.

She wants to have children of her own as the mother has done and some time ago started to show interest in how babies are born. When she was told the facts, she was "absolutely thrilled." She has since "longed to be married and have a baby" but was dismayed when she learned that it was customary for men to propose to women asking, "Who will ask me to marry them?"

Much of what would have previously been gross attempts at phallic exhibitionism have become transformed in an interest in her looks, wanting to use lipstick, and in a more sublimated form of exhibitionism of the whole body, as can be seen by her graceful dancing whenever she hears music. This transformation of the phallic exhibitionistic attempts characteristic of the phallic-oedipal position, first stage, to a cathexis and an interest in the whole body and whatever may embellish it is one of the many necessary steps to be taken in developmental line from the active-masculine position to the passive-feminine one.

During the interview with the psychiatrist she gave further evidence of the many feminine identifications she has already established, such as when she showed her fascination with the small cooker, kettle, etc., in the corner of the room where she was being interviewed.

It is possible to discern from the diagnostic interviews that she has reached the second stage, the oedipal stage, and that her oedipal constellation is essentially a positive one, that is, she has not only taken the father as an object but has done so essentially from a passive-feminine position.

Three groups of factors require further comment. First, there is still some phallic (clitoridal) activity. It is perfectly possible of course that this is the expression of some still active remnants of the previous masculine, phallic-oedipal stage, or of some degree of fixation to it. Yet it is not really feasible to decide this question without an exact knowledge of the fantasies (and the role she plays in them) that accompany her occasional masturbation.

If these fantasies were of a passive-feminine character one could not conclude that the girl's sexual position is a masculine one. In fact, in my view (as we saw earlier) this may well be a normal stage, the stage where the clitoris remains an excitable erotogenic zone but the accompanying fantasies have lost most of their masculine character.

Second, though in her case history there are clear signs of oral fixation that belong especially in the relationship to the mother (pre-phallic elements) and influence it they do not seem in her case to have unduly interfered with her move into the second stage of her oedipal development. In other words, they have not determined, as may happen occasionally in such cases, a fixation to the phallic-oedipal (first stage) relationship to the mother. Third, the positive oedipal manifestations, second stage, are particularly overt and quite open when she is compared with most girls of nearly six.

Appendix

Recent Embryological, Anatomical and
Physiological Findings

Embryological Findings

Sherfey (1973) has pointed out how modern embryological research shows that the earlier theories of a bisexual origin embryo are apparently incorrect. These theories had assumed that both the masculine and feminine embryological precursors of the sexual organs were simultaneously present in the embryo. Final determination depended on the development of either the masculine or feminine element with the concomitant atrophy of its counterpart. Such anatomical residues as the verumontanum in the male were assumed to be the atrophic remnants of the feminine organs. Similarly, the clitoris, for example, was considered the atrophic residue in the female of structures that would have developed into a penis in the case of masculine development. Such theories were taught in many medical schools as late as the nineteen forties. Modern embryological formulations claim that all mammalian embryos (of later males and females) are anatomically female to start with. The differentiation of a male from this initial female matrix is due to androgen hormones and is usually completed by about the twelfth week of fetal life.

Much has been made by a number of authors of these facts.

Anatomical and Physiological Findings

Masters and Johnson (1966) clarified the anatomy and physiology of sexual intercourse.

The all important labial-preputial-glandar mechanism maintains continuous stimulation (essential for a female orgasm) of the glans of the clitoris by the prepuce during intravaginal coition. This is achieved by the thrusting movement of the penis in the vagina which are then transmitted, thanks to the labial-glandar-mechanism, to the clitoris' prepuce leading to a rhythmic rubbing of the clitoris by the edematous prepuce until the degree of excitation required for the orgastic discharge is achieved.

Masters and Johnson have further demonstrated that women are capable of repeated orgasms in quick succession under appropriate conditions while for the male there is usually a refractory period of about half an hour before a second ejaculation and orgasm can be achieved. It is said that as many as six orgasms are possible for the female during sexual intercourse, while by means of direct clitoral stimulation as many as fifty orgasms can be obtained in a period of an hour, if actual physical exhaustion does not intervene.

Sherfey (1973) has discussed those physical-anatomical factors that she believes lead to frigidity during sexual intercourse by interfering with the mechanism just described. She believes that such factors may well be primarily responsible for a large percentage of actual cases of frigidity, without in any way denying the importance of psychological factors, cultural pressures, etc.

The Concept of the Complementary Series

As I see it, Freud's concept of the complementary series is quite applicable here. At the one extreme of the continuum there are the cases where anatomo-biological factors are essentially responsible for frigidity (some examples of which are to be described below), while at the other lie those cases where it is essentially psychological issues, neurotic and emotional problems, sociocultural or religious factors, etc., that can be blamed for the absence of the orgasm. In between these two extremes there lie all those cases in which the frigid response can be explained by a combination, in variable proportions, of biological and psychological determinants.

Pregnancy and Orgastic Capacity

It is a well-known clinical fact that some women's orgastic capacity does not appear frequently until after their first or second pregnancy. Sherfey (1973) theorizes that pregnancies enhance the sexual function by means of the hormonal flooding that takes place during this period. She believes that such flooding determines an enormous growth and vascularization of the pelvic structures, including varicosities that she considers both nonadaptive and adaptive. On the one hand, they are minor residues of pathological developments due to the pregnancy. On the other hand, given the fact that the orgasm is produced by the sudden and massive vasoconstriction on the engorged pelvic structures, pregnancy enhances the orgastic capacity through the increased vascularization. She believes this explains the orgastic difficulties of adolescent females that mature late and retain a somewhat juvenile pelvic condition until after their first or second pregnancies. She remarks that in such women only a simple bulbar orgasm by means of manual masturbation is possible.

Obstetrical Damage and Orgastic Capacity

Sherfey (1973) points out that without obstetrical care excessive obstetrical damage to the female sex organs takes place in nearly 100 percent of women delivering their first child. Even with good obstetrical care it takes place very frequently indeed.

Tears of the perineum, especially of the vestibular bulbs and their muscles, are usually unilateral and according to Sherfey have the capacity to significantly diminish the orgasmic reaction. Among the reasons is the subsequent interference with the labial-preputial-glandar mechanism. Tears of the perineal muscles themselves are, according to Sherfey, one of the most common causes of frigidity during later sexual intercourse, in part because they may leave a very widened vaginal orifice. When this is the case, the increase in localized engorgement in the vaginal plexus and bulb that tightens the lower third of the vagina around the penis cannot occur (the tightening around the penis will not take place). Since this tightening is important for the utmost efficiency of the labial-preputial-glandar mechanism, the final increase in sexual excitation to trigger the orgastic response will fail to take place in spite of the fact that pelvic congestion and edema are at an appropriate level.

Sherfey rightly pointed out that mild degrees of perineal damage are likely to go unnoticed since the widening of the vaginal orifice may not be too marked, yet will interfere with the orgastic response. Such cases may no doubt be mistaken for psychogenic frigidity.

Sherfey's arguments are in my view convincing enough to demand that a good gynecological examination be part of any psychiatric evaluation of the causes of the frigidity in any given case. The complementary series concepts already referred to should be very valuable in arriving at a more precise diagnostic formulation of the causative factors.

Furthermore, as Sherfey points out, there is the whole issue of the variations and anomalies of the anatomy of the female sexual organs that may well interfere with or, on occasion, totally preclude the orgasm.

Functional Factors

Given that all is well in the anatomo-physiological sense, there still remains the fact that, for the female orgasm to take place, appropriate physical stimulation in terms of quantity, quality, and length of time, is a *sine qua non*. As Sherfey (1973) and many others point out, inadequate erotogenic stimulation is unquestionably the most frequent cause of vaginal frigidity.

As Masters and Johnson (1966) and Kinsey (1953) have pointed out, sexual excitation and tension in the female diminish instantly if stimulation is stopped.

Given that the amount of stimulation required by many women is well in excess of the amount of time that many men can maintain an erection without an ejaculation, we have a readymade problem. Women seem to need "normally" (under present societal conditions) a longer arousal time than their male sexual partners.

The Role of Culture, Fantasies and Other
Psychic Stimuli

The reasons for this disparity between males and females are not well known or understood, and there is much debate around the subject. There are those, such as Kinsey (1953) who postulated a type of biological "cerebral" difference between men and women. Presumably, he was led to this by finding that approximately 75 percent of men ejaculate in about two minutes after penetration, while many women require about ten minutes of penile stimulation before reaching orgasm. (This time seems less nowadays than it was in 1953. The figures more frequently given are a minimum of four to six minutes.) He had linked this with his finding that there was an enormous disparity in the response to sexual psychic stimulation between males and females. He thought that men, in contrast to women, were very responsive to sexual thoughts, fantasies, expectations, etc. This helps to keep them stimulated and erected even during coital interruptions while the female is dependent on constant, rhythmic tactile stimulation or her sexual tension disappears.

More recently, Schmidt et al. (1973) found this disparity regarding psychic stimulation in males and females to be incorrect, and linked it instead with sociocultural attitudes toward sexuality, child-rearing practices, etc., that tended to inhibit female sexual expressions and responsiveness to this kind of stimuli. Thus ego and superego ideals were developed that limited the female response and very frequently made it highly conflictual.

In 1974 Stanley called attention to the fact that the disparity between males and females in the time required to reach a climax is a response pattern that is not physiological. She pointed out the fact that males and females respond to masturbation within a period of one to three minutes. She asked the very legitimate question: "What accounts for the difference in intercourse?"

She took the position that inhibitions related to long-standing guilt about sex may be highly influential, and cultural attitudes which link woman's sexuality inextricably to feelings of trust and affection as a necessary precondition to a successful sexual life. She argued for broadening the realm of what may be considered psychically sexually stimulating for women (beyond Kinsey's criteria), concluding that it "may now seem more possible that breaks in physical stimulation could be adequately compensated for by accompanying psychological stimuli, with no resulting diminution in women's sexual arousal" (p. 11). This is particularly so, in her view (and that of others), because in the twenty years intervening since Kinsey's report, women have acquired "permission" from society to be more sexually responsive and expressive.

I most certainly agree with Stanley about the fundamental importance of the psychological attitudes, sociocultural patterns and other emotional difficulties that contribute frequently to a maladaptive sexual function in females. Yet I believe that the concept of the complementary series, as described above, is the more rational basis for a diagnostic, prognostic and therapeutic approach to the problem.

BIBLIOGRAPHY

Abraham, K. (1920), Manifestations of the female castration complex. *Selected Papers*. London: Hogarth Press, 1927. P. 388.

Bonaparte, M. (1953), *Female Sexuality*. London: Imago Publishing Co.

Brierly, M. (1932), Some problems of integration in women. *International Journal of Psycho-Analysis*, 13:443-48.

Deutsch, H. (1925), The psychology of women in relation to the function of reproduction. *The Psychoanalytic Reader*. London: Hogarth Press, 1950.

———— (1930), The significance of masochism in the mental life of women. *International Journal of Psycho-Analysis*, 11:48.

———— (1932), On female homosexuality. *Psychoanalytic Quarterly*, 1:484.

Eissler, K. (1939), On certain problems of female sexual development. *Psychoanalytic Quarterly*, 8:191-210. Quote, p. 206.

Fenichel, O. (1932), The pregenital antecedents of the oedipus complex. *International Journal of Psycho-Analysis*, 12:141.

Flügel, J. C. (1925), A note on the phallic significance of the tongue. *International Journal of Psycho-Analysis*, 6:209.

Freud, A. (1965), *Normality and Pathology in Childhood*. New York: International Universities Press. Pp. 187-88.

Freud, S. (1897), Letter 64 to Fliess, May 31, 1897, and letter 71, October 15, 1897. *The Origins of Psychoanalysis*. Eds. Marie Bonaparte, Anna Freud, and Ernest Kris. London: Imago Publishing Co., 1954. Pp. 206, 221.

———— (1899), Letter 113 to Fliess, August 1, 1899. *The Origins of Psychoanalysis*. London: Imago Publishing Co., 1954. P. 288.

———— (1900), *The Interpretation of Dreams*. Standard Ed., 4:263.

———— (1905), *Three Essays in the Theory of Sexuality*. Standard Ed., 7:220.

———— (1910), A special type of choice of object made by men. Standard Ed., 11:171.

———— (1915), Instincts and their vicissitudes. Standard Ed., 14:122.

———— (1916-17), *Introductory Lectures. Standard Ed.*, 15:207, 16:307.

———— (1918 [1914]), From the history of an infantile neurosis. Standard Ed., 17:119.

———— (1919), A child is being beaten. Standard Ed., 17:179.

———— (1923a), *The Ego and the Id*. Standard Ed., 17:33-34.

———— (1923b), The infantile genital organization of the libido. Standard Ed., 19:145.

137

—— (1924c), The economic problem of masochism. Standard Ed., 19:157-73.

—— (1924d), The dissolution of the oedipus complex. Standard Ed., 19:178.

—— (1925), Some psychological consequences of the anatomical distinction between the sexes. Standard Ed., 19:256.

—— (1931), Female sexuality. Standard Ed., 21:225.

Gittelson, M. (1952), Re-evaluation of the role of the oedipus complex. *International Journal of Psycho-Analysis*, 33:351-54.

Greenacre, P. (1950), Special problems of early female development. *Psychoanalytic Study of the Child*, 5:112-38.

Horney, K. (1924), On the genesis of the castration complex in women. *International Journal of Psycho-Analysis*, 5:50.

—— (1926), The flight from womanhood. *International Journal of Psycho-Analysis*, 7:324.

—— (1933), The denial of the vagina. *International Journal of Psycho-Analysis*, 14:57-70.

James, M. (1960), Premature ego development: some observations upon disturbances in the first three years of life. *International Journal of Psycho-Analysis*, 41:288-95.

Jones, E. (1923), *Essays in Applied Psychoanalysis*. London: International Psychoanalytic Press. Pp. 304-12.

—— (1927), The early development of female sexuality. *International Journal of Psycho-Analysis*, 8:459-72.

—— (1935), Early female sexuality. *International Journal of Psycho-Analysis*, 16:264, 270.

Kestenberg, J. (1956a), Vicissitudes of female sexuality. *Journal of the American Psychoaanalytic Association*, 4:453-76.

—— (1956b), On the development of maternal feelings in early childhood: observations and reflections. *Psychoanalytic Study of the Child*, 11:256-91.

Kinsey, A. C., et al. (1953), *Sexual Behavior in the Human Female*. Philadelphia: Saunders.

Klein, M. (1932), *The Psychoanalysis of Children*. London: Hogarth Press.

Lampl de Groot, J. (1928), The evolution of the oedipus complex in women. *International Journal of Psycho-Analysis*, 9:332.

—— (1946), The pre-oedipal phase in the development of the male child. *Psychoanalytic Study of the Child*, 2:75-113.

—— (1952), Re-evaluation of the role of the oedipus complex. *International of Psycho-Analysis*, 33:1-8.

Loewenstein, R. (1935), Phallic passivity in men. *International Journal of Psycho-Analysis*, 16:337.

Mack Brunswick, R. (1940), The preoedipal phase of the libido development. *The Psychoanalytic Reader*. London: Hogarth Press, 1950.

Masters, W., and Johnson, V. (1966), *Human Sexual Responses*. Boston: Little, Brown.

Moore, B. E. (1964), Frigidity: a review of psychoanalytic literature. *Psychoanalytic Quarterly*, 33:323-49.

Müller, J. (1932), A contribution to the problem of libidinal development of the genital phase in girls. *International Journal of Psycho-Analysis*, 13:362-68.

Nagera, H. (1963), The developmental profile: notes on its clinical applications. *Psychoanalytic Study of the Child*, 18:511.

———— (1964a), Autoeroticism, autoerotic activities and ego development. *Psychoanalytic Study of the Child,* 19:240.

———— (1964b), On arrest in development, fixation and regression. *Psychoanalytic Study of the Child,* 19:222.

———— (1966), *Early Childhood Disturbances, the Infantile Neurosis and the Adulthood Disturbances: Problems of a Developmental Psychoanalytic Psychology.* New York: International Universities Press. Monograph No. 2 of *The Psychoanalytic Study of the Child.*

Rado, S. (1933), Fear of castration in women. *Psychoanalytic Quarterly,* 2:425-75.

Schmidt, G., and Sigusch, V. (1973), Women's sexual arousal. *Contemporary Sexual Behavior: Critical Issues in the 1970's.* Eds. J. Zubin and J. Money. Baltimore:

————, and Schäfer, S. (1973), Responses to reading erotic stories: male-female differences. *Archives of Sexual Behavior,* 2:181.

Sherfey, M. J. (1966), The evolution and nature of female sexuality in relation to psychoanalytic theory. *Journal of the American Psychoanalytic Association,* 14:28-129.

———— (1973), On the nature of female sexuality. *Psychoanalysis and Women.* Ed. J. Baker Miller. New York: Brunner/Mazel. Pp. 136-54.

Stanley, J. (1974), *Medical Aspects of Human Sexuality.* New York: Hospital Publications.

Van der Leeuw, P. J. (1958), The preoedipal phase of the male. *Psychoanalytic Study of the Child,* 13:352-75.

INDEX

Abraham, K., 3
acting out, 89
active-feminine position, 36
active-masculine position, viii, 7, 12, 15-16, 22-23, 27, 35, 42, 44-46, 48, 49, 53, 54, 56-58, 63, 64, 73-76, 108-109, 113, 123, 124, 129
active oedipus complex, 1-2, 21, 38
anal intercourse, 46n, 47n, 67, 69, 84-85, 98
anal phase, 6, 9, 12, 18, 19, 26, 27, 29, 31, 59-60, 67, 107, 109, 110, 122
    sadistic, 33-34, 65, 67, 69, 72, 75-77
androgen hormones, 131
anorexia nervosa, 106
anus, 30
autoeroticism, 32, 50, 72; see also masturbation; masturbatory fantasies

Bartholin glands, 51
Basic Psychoanalytic Concepts on the Libido Theory (Nagera), 2n
bedwetting, 78, 105
bisexuality:
    in children, 4, 5, 10, 12, 13, 15, 16, 19, 21, 30, 42-44, 48, 53n, 55-58, 63, 64, 127
    in embryo, 131
Bonaparte, M., 37-39, 45, 52n, 120
breast, 57
Brierly, M., 50n
bust development, 83, 90

castration, 39, 74, 76, 85, 122
    anxiety, 26, 27, 30, 114
Child Psychoanalytic Study Program (University of Michigan), 115, 120
childbirth, 75, 76

Clinical Concept Research Group (Hampstead Clinic), vii, ix
clitoris, 10, 12, 38, 39, 42, 45, 47, 49, 50, 52-56, 60, 62, 74-76, 121, 122, 130, 131
coitus, *see* sexual intercourse
complementary series, 132, 136
complete oedipus complex, 4, 5

Dansky, E., 33n
death wishes, 33, 106-107
defensive reinforcement, 20
depression, postpartum, 79, 106, 109
desexualization, viii
Deutsch, H., 44, 49, 50n
Diagnostic Profile (Hampstead Clinic), vii, ix
divorce, 24, 85, 87, 89, 93, 107

education, 80-81, 83, 87, 88
Ego and the Id, The (S. Freud), 3
ego attitudes, 14-15, 24, 26, 40, 58, 63
ego development, viii, 13, 20, 43, 48, 59-67, 74, 115
ego ideals, 135
ego identification, viii, 24, 37, 40, 57, 63, 64, 75, 76, 84, 108, 113, 117
Eissler, K., 50n
ejaculation, 132, 134, 135
embryo, 56, 131
erotogenic zone, vii, viii, 12, 23, 24, 31-32, 42, 47, 53, 54, 59-60, 74-76, 130
exhibitionism, 122, 129

fantasies, 7, 13, 22, 24, 29-30, 31, 35, 37, 45, 47n, 50-53, 58, 61, 63, 65-67, 69, 70, 72-76, 81, 83-85, 88, 91-95, 99, 100-104, 107-108, 115, 117, 119, 122, 125, 127-130, 135; *see also* masturbatory fantasies; prostitution, fantasies of

141

DATE			
NOV 2 9 1980			
FEB - 3 1986			
MAY 2 2 1987			
AUG 1 2 1987			
MAY 2 6 1995			
JAN 0 2 1996			
SEP 1 1 1997			
APR 1 1 1998			